English Folk Tales

Level 1
(1000-word)

Retold by Emma Sully

IBC パブリッシング

はじめに

　ラダーシリーズは、「はしご (ladder)」を使って一歩一歩上を目指すように、学習者の実力に合わせ、無理なくステップアップできるよう開発された英文リーダーのシリーズです。

　リーディング力をつけるためには、繰り返したくさん読むこと、いわゆる「多読」がもっとも効果的な学習法であると言われています。多読では、「1. 速く 2. 訳さず英語のまま 3. なるべく辞書を使わず」に読むことが大切です。スピードを計るなど、速く読むよう心がけましょう（たとえば TOEIC® テストの音声スピードはおよそ 1 分間に 150 語です）。そして 1 語ずつ訳すのではなく、英語を英語のまま理解するくせをつけるようにします。こうして読み続けるうちに語感がついてきて、だんだんと英語が理解できるようになるのです。まずは、ラダーシリーズの中からあなたのレベルに合った本を選び、少しずつ英文に慣れ親しんでください。たくさんの本を手にとるうちに、英文書がすらすら読めるようになってくるはずです。

《本シリーズの特徴》
- 中学校レベルから中級者レベルまで5段階に分かれています。自分に合ったレベルからスタートしてください。
- クラシックから現代文学、ノンフィクション、ビジネスと幅広いジャンルを扱っています。あなたの興味に合わせてタイトルを選べます。
- 巻末のワードリストで、いつでもどこでも単語の意味を確認できます。レベル1、2では、文中の全ての単語が、レベル3以上は中学校レベル外の単語が掲載されています。
- カバーにヘッドホンマークのついているタイトルは、オーディオ・サポートがあります。ウェブから購入／ダウンロードし、リスニング教材としても併用できます。

《使用語彙について》
レベル1：中学校で学習する単語約1000語
レベル2：レベル1の単語＋使用頻度の高い単語約300語
レベル3：レベル1の単語＋使用頻度の高い単語約600語
レベル4：レベル1の単語＋使用頻度の高い単語約1000語
レベル5：語彙制限なし

Contents

Some Merry Tales of
 the Wise Men of Gotham...............1

The Story of
 the Three Little Pigs.......................19

Jack and the Beanstalk..........................31

The History of
 Jack and the Giants.......................65

Word List..100

Some Merry Tales of the Wise Men of Gotham

読みはじめる前に

Some Merry Tales of the Wise Men of Gotham で使われている用語です。わからない語は巻末のワードリストで確認しましょう。

- ☐ tale
- ☐ sheep
- ☐ neighbor
- ☐ Lent
- ☐ feast
- ☐ eel
- ☐ drown
- ☐ baptize
- ☐ godparent
- ☐ priest

あらすじ

ゴッサムはイギリスのノッティンガムシャー地方に実在する村の名前です。英語で「ゴッサムの賢人」といえば、おろか者の代名詞なのです。

橋の通行権でもめる村人の話、鳥の飼育方法を考えた村人の話、市場にチーズを売りに行く村人の話、残った魚をどうするか考えた村人の話、釣り場で仲間が一人足りないことに気づいた村人の話、赤ん坊の名付け親を務める村の子どもたちの話など、ゴッサム村の人々のおどろくほどの「賢人ぶり」が楽しい6つの短編です。

The First Tale

Two men from the city of Gotham met on Nottingham bridge. One man, Peter, was on his way back from the market. The other man, John, was going to the market to buy sheep.

"Hello, where are you going?" asked Peter.

"I am going to the market to buy sheep," said John.

"Buy sheep?" asked Peter. "Which way will you bring them home?"

"I will bring them over this bridge," said John.

"No, you will not!" said Peter.

"Yes, I will!" said John.

"No, you will not!" said Peter.

"Yes, I will," said John.

The two continued to fight in this way, back and forth. They got so angry, they began to beat their wooden canes against the bridge.

"You may not bring them over this bridge," said Peter.

"I do not care what you say," said John. "I will bring them over this bridge. They will all come this way!"

As the men fought, another man, who was wiser than Peter and John, came from the market. He carried a large bag of food. He heard Peter and John fighting, and he wanted to teach them a lesson.

"Why are you fighting? You are both very foolish. Will you never learn? Help me," he said. "Help me put this bag of food over my shoulder."

Peter and John stopped fighting, and they went to the man with the food. They both helped him lift the heavy bag onto his back so that the bag went over his shoulder.

"Thank you," said the man. As Peter and John watched, the man walked over to the edge of the bridge. Slowly, he took the bag of food off of his back, opened the bag, and emptied all of the food out of the bag into the river.

"How much food is left in this bag, my

friends?" asked the man.

"What have you done?" asked Peter.

"What have you done?" asked John.

"There is no food left in the bag," they both said together.

"You two men have as much sense as the food left in this bag," said the man. Peter and John looked at each other, and the man on the bridge walked away.

The Second Tale

Once upon a time, the men of Gotham found a special bird. These men wanted the beautiful bird to sing to them all year. They decided to build a place to keep the bird. In the center of town, they planted small trees in a circle. They put the special bird in the middle of the circle and said to her—

"Sing here, bird, and we will give you all the food and drink you need, all year long."

The bird, being smarter than the men, looked at them, looked at the sky, and flew away.

"Oh no!" said the men. "We did not plant tall enough trees!"

The Third Tale

A man of Gotham went to Nottingham Market to sell his cheese. As he walked into town, one of his cheeses fell out of his hand and rolled down the hill.

"Oh no!" said the man. "Surely you can't go to the market alone!" he said to his cheese. "I will send another along to help you!"

He took another cheese out of his pocket, and he dropped it so that it, too, would roll down the hill.

Both cheeses rolled down the hill, one after another.

"Meet me at the market!" he shouted to his cheese.

The man continued into town and came to the market. He waited and waited for his cheese. The cheese did not come. He asked the neighbors and other men if they had seen his cheese.

"Who is bringing your cheese?" asked one of the neighbors.

"Why, they are bringing themselves! They knew the way," the man said.

"Though perhaps they went farther than the market. Maybe they are in York!"

The man got on his horse, and he began to travel to York. He arrived at York, and still he could not find his cheese. To this day, no one has ever heard from the cheese.

The Fourth Tale

During Lent, the good men of Gotham feasted on fish. When Good Friday came, they had many fish left over. There were big fish and small fish, white fish and red fish. They did not know what to do with them. They talked and they talked, and they agreed that if they put their fish into the pond in the middle of town, perhaps by next year, they would have even more fish during Lent.

"Next year, when Lent comes, we will eat like kings!" they cried.

The next year, at the beginning of Lent, they went to the pond. They thought they would find hundreds of fish. They looked in the pond, and they were surprised to see no fish at all, only a large eel.

"Oh no!" they cried. "This terrible eel has eaten all of our fish!"

"What should we do?" asked one man.

"Kill him!" another one said.

"Cut him up!" said another.

"No," said another. "Let's drown him."

"Yes, let's drown him!" they agreed.

They went to another pond and threw the eel into the water.

The Fifth Tale

Twelve men from Gotham went fishing. Some went into the water, and some stayed on land. When they went home, one said to another, "We had this wonderful day by the water. I am glad that none of us drowned."

Each man counted the men around them. Each man counted 11 men, not 12.

"Oh no!" said one man. "One of us did drown! There are now only 11 men."

The men went back to the fishing spot. They looked for their friend. They were very sad. A man rode by on a horse and saw the group of men. "Why are you so sad?" he asked.

"We came here to fish," one of them said. "And one of us drowned here!"

"How many of you came to fish?" the man asked.

"12 of us came, and now there are only 11 of us," they said.

"What will you give me if I find you your 12th man?

"Sir," they said. "We will give you all of the money that we have."

"Give me your money," said the man. He walked around to all of the men, put his hands on their shoulders, and counted out loud. Sure enough, there were 12 men.

"Thank god," said the men. "You found our dear brother!"

The Sixth Tale

In Gotham, a man's wife had a child. The child was to be baptized, and the father needed godparents for the child. The father called in children who were between the ages of 8 and 10 years old. The oldest child, who was to be the godfather, was named Gilbert. The second child was Humphrey. The third child, who was to be the godmother, was Christabel. The children's friends told them they must listen to the priest, who would baptize the child.

"Do you all agree on the baby's

name?" asked the priest.

"Do you all agree on the baby's name?" asked Gilbert.

The priest then said, "Where do you come from?"

Gilbert said, "Where do you come from?"

Humphrey said, "Where do you come from?"

And Christabel said, "Where do you come from?"

The priest was so surprised he did not know what to say. He whistled, and said "Whew!"

Gilbert whistled and said, "Whew!" Humphrey whistled and said, "Whew!" and so did Christabel.

This made the priest very angry. So he said, "Go home, fools, go home!"

You can guess what Gilbert, Humphrey, and Christabel said.

The priest then decided that he would find godparents for the child himself.

The Story of the Three Little Pigs

読みはじめる前に

The Story of the Three Little Pigs で使われている用語です。わからない語は巻末のワードリストで確認しましょう。

- ☐ bundle
- ☐ straw
- ☐ chinny-chin-chin
- ☐ blow
- ☐ brick
- ☐ scared
- ☐ fair
- ☐ chimney

あらすじ

あるところにお母さんブタと、3匹の子ブタがいました。3匹の子ブタたちは家を出て独立するにあたり、それぞれ家を建てることにしました。ワラ、小枝、レンガなど、3匹とも違う素材で家を作ります。すると一匹のオオカミが子ブタたちの新築の家を訪れ、「中に入れておくれ」と言うのです。もちろん子ブタたちはお断りするのですが……。

Once an old mother pig lived with her three little pigs. She did not have enough money to take care of them, so she sent them out to live on their own.

The first pig that went out met a man who had a bundle of straw. "Please, sir, may I have that straw so that I can build a house?" The man gave the pig the straw, and the little pig built a house.

Soon a mean wolf came along. He knocked on the pig's door. "Little pig, little pig, let me come in," he said.

"Not by the hair of my chinny-chin-chin," said the pig.

"Then I'll blow your house down!" said the wolf. The wolf blew and blew, and the house fell down. He ate the little pig up.

The second pig walked into town, and on his way, he met a man with a bundle of sticks. "Please, sir, may I have those sticks so that I can build a house?" The man gave the pig the sticks, and the pig went to build his house.

The wolf then came along to the second pig's house, and said, "Little pig, little pig, let me come in."

"Not by the hair of my chinny-chin-chin," said the pig.

"Then I'll blow your house down!" The wolf blew and blew. At last, he blew the house down, and he ate the second pig.

The third little pig met a man who was carrying a large pile of bricks. "Please, sir," said the little pig. "May I have those bricks so that I can build a house?" The man agreed to give the bricks to the pig, and off the pig went to make his brick house.

Can you guess what happened next? The wolf came to the third pig's brick house. "Little pig, little pig, let me come in," he said.

"Not by the hair of my chinny-chin-chin," said the pig.

"Then I'll blow your house down."

The wolf blew and blew, but no matter how hard he blew, he could not blow down the little pig's brick house.

"Little pig," the wolf said.

"Yes," said the pig, from inside the house.

"I know where there is a field of potatoes," said the wolf.

"Where?" said the little Pig.

"At Mr. Smith's. Do you want to go there with me tomorrow morning? I will come and get you, if you'd like to go."

"Ok," said the little pig. "I will be ready. What time will you come?"

"Six o'clock," said the wolf.

"Ok. I will be ready," said the pig. The little pig was very smart, and he knew better than to wait for the wolf. So he woke up at five in the morning, went to get the potatoes, and was home before six.

At six o'clock, he heard someone at his door.

"Are you ready, little pig?" asked the wolf.

"Am I ready?" said the little pig. "I sure am! I already went to get the potatoes! And I am already cooking them for dinner."

The wolf was very angry, but he decided to try another idea. "Little pig," said the wolf. "I know where we can find a nice apple tree."

"Where?" said the Pig.

"At Merry Garden," said the wolf. "I do not want you to trick me again, though. I will come at five o'clock tomorrow, and we will go together to get some apples."

The little pig got up very, very early at four in the morning, and he set off to get the apples. It was farther than the potato field, though, so as he was climbing down from the apple tree, he saw the wolf.

"Little pig!" said the wolf. "Why are you here before me? How are the apples?"

"They are very nice," said the little pig. "I will throw one down to you." The little pig threw the apple very far. The wolf ran to go get it, and the pig decided that was the right moment to climb down the tree and run back home. The pig ran away safely.

The next day, the wolf was back. "Little pig," said the wolf. "There is a fair in town. Do you want to go?"

"Oh, yes," said the pig. "At what time will you be ready?"

"At three," said the wolf.

As before, the little pig set off one hour before they were going to meet. He got to the fair and bought a butter maker. On his way home, he saw the wolf. "I better hide!" thought the pig. He turned the butter maker on its side, and it began to roll down the hill with the pig inside. It rolled and rolled very fast, and it rolled right past the wolf. The wolf was scared, and he ran home without going to the fair.

The wolf went instead to the little pig's house. "I was so scared today! I was walking to the fair, and this big round thing rolled down the hill, right past me!"

The little pig was so happy he had scared the wolf, he said, "Ha ha! I scared you! I went to the fair and bought this butter maker. I saw you, got into it, and rolled down the hill!"

This made the wolf so angry that he said, "I am going to eat you up! I am going to come down your chimney."

The pig thought quickly. He put a pot of water in the fireplace and lit a fire. The wolf came down the chimney and fell into the pot of very hot water! The pig put the lid on the pot, cooked the wolf, and ate him for dinner.

Jack and the Beanstalk

読みはじめる前に

Jack and the Beanstalk で使われている用語です。わからない語は巻末のワードリストで確認しましょう。

☐ beanstalk　　☐ giant　　　☐ stab
☐ cow　　　　　☐ treasure　　☐ hen
☐ butcher　　　☐ steal　　　☐ disguise
☐ stalk　　　　☐ servant

あらすじ

ジャックは母と二人、ロンドンから遠く離れた田舎で細々と暮らしていました。食べるものも尽き、母親はとうとう最後の財産である牛も売ることにしました。ところがジャックは、その大切な牛をわずかの豆と交換してしまったのです！

怒った母親が豆を庭に打ち捨てると、豆はみるみる成長し、天高くつるを伸ばしました。ジャックは心配する母親を残し、つるを登って空の国へ出かけていきます。そこで、思いがけない家族の過去を知ることになるのです。

Once upon a time, a poor woman lived in a little house many, many miles away from London. Her husband died, and she and her only child, Jack, lived together. Jack meant everything to the poor woman, and because he was all that she had, she gave him everything that he wanted. If he wanted more food, she gave him more food. If he wanted more clothes, she bought him more clothes. As a result, Jack thought of no one but himself. Since Jack wanted many things, they quickly ran out of all that they had.

They became very poor, and as time went on, the only thing that they had left was a cow.

Jack's mother was not sure how they would live, or how they would have money for food. She was very upset. One day, she went to Jack crying. She got angry at him for the first time in her life. "You terrible boy! You terrible, terrible boy! Because of you, we have nothing left! We have no money for food. The only thing we have left is our cow. Now I must sell our cow, too, because we have to eat."

Jack asked if he could sell the cow. She wanted to sell it herself, but finally she agreed to let Jack sell it. Jack headed to the village with the cow. He and the cow walked for a little while until Jack came to a butcher. The butcher asked where he was bringing the cow. "I am selling the cow," Jack said.

Jack could see that the butcher held some strange beans in his hand. The beans were such bright colors that Jack saw them right away. The butcher saw Jack look at the beans, and he knew he could get Jack to give him the cow for the beans. "I will buy the cow from you," the butcher said. "I can pay you with these magic beans instead of money."

Jack was a very foolish boy, and he believed the butcher when the butcher told Jack that the beans were magic. Right away, Jack agreed to sell the cow for the magic beans. Jack walked home and was excited to surprise his mother.

His mother could not believe her eyes. Where was their money? What had Jack done? How could he have sold their cow for beans? Now they would have no food. Now they did not even have their cow! They had nothing. She was so angry that she shouted, and she kicked the beans out of Jack's hands. The beans flew into the air. They landed all over their house, and some even went so far that they landed out in their garden. Jack cried, and his mother cried. They went to bed hungry, for they had no food. All that they had were some magic beans.

Jack woke up, as he did every

morning. But something was different. He looked out his window, and he saw a large green stalk. Some of the beans in the garden had started to grow! He went outside to look at the stalk more closely. The plant was unusual. It was not small, which is what you would expect on the first day a plant grows. It was very, very large. The stalk was so thick and tall that it looked like he could climb it up into the sky.

He went outside to take a closer look. The beanstalk was so tall he could not even see its top. He put his hand on the stalk, and it seemed strong enough for him to climb. "These certainly are magic beans," he thought. He decided he would climb to the top. He went inside to tell his mother his plan. He was sure she would be happy that the beans were magic, after all. She cried to him, "No, Jack! Do not go!" The beanstalk made her nervous, and she did not want to lose her boy, but she could not change Jack's mind. He decided to climb the beanstalk anyway.

Jack climbed and climbed for hours. He was very, very tired. He finally reached the top, looked around,

and saw a strange country. There was nothing around him. He did not see trees, or plants, or animals. There were no houses at all. There were definitely no people. The only thing he saw were some small rocks. Jack sat on a rock in the middle of this strange place in the sky, and he felt very sad as he thought of his mother, who he left alone. He thought about what she would be doing, and if she was sad that he was gone. He wondered if he would die from being so hungry up here in this land in the sky.

After resting for a little while, he walked on in search of something to eat or drink. Far away, he saw a young woman. She was beautiful and wore a very pretty dress. She had a small, white wand in her hand.

She came over to Jack. Jack was not sure if she would be nice, so he stayed where he was as she walked over to him. She asked Jack nicely, "How did you get here?"

Jack told her the story of the beanstalk. He told her how he lived alone with his mother because his father had died. He even told her how he did not know his father, and that his mother would never answer his questions about his father. Whenever he mentioned his father, his mother would only cry, and she would be upset for days. He said he always felt like his father's death was something that he and his mother could never talk about. He knew better than to ask her questions.

"I can tell you everything you need to know about your father," the woman said. "But before I begin, you must promise to do everything I ask you to. I am a fairy. If you do not do as you promise, you will be destroyed."

Jack was scared, and he agreed to her wishes.

"Your father was very rich," the fairy said. "He was a very good man, too. He used his money to take care of the poor. He helped everyone around him. He wanted to bring other people happiness. He made a promise to do good every single day, and he lived his life by this promise. There was a terrible giant who lived very far away. This giant was as bad a person as your father was good. The giant was also very poor. He heard about your father, and how rich your father was, and so he decided to see if he could steal your father's money and treasures. When your father met the giant, he of course helped him, because your father helped everyone, whether they were a person or a giant. Your father gave the giant a place to live, and he gave him food.

"During the time that the giant lived near your father, he spent much of his time thinking about how he could steal all of your father's riches. One day when there was a lot of rain, the giant saw in the distance some ships that were in danger because of the terrible weather. He told your father that he should send his servants to help the people on the boats. Your father agreed, and he sent every person who worked for him off to help the ships. No one was left at your house except the giant and your father, and you and your mother were at the other end of the large house. When the giant was alone with your father in your father's office, he took a knife and stabbed your father.

"You were 3 months old. Because you and your mother were in a different part of the house, she did not know what had happened. When she went into the office, she found your father dead. She was very, very scared. Your mother saw the giant, and she begged him to let you and her live.

"For a moment, the giant seemed to feel bad about what he had done. He agreed to let you both live. But first, he made her promise never to tell you who your father was or answer any questions about him. He said if your mother told you anything, he would kill you both. Your mother ran away from him. The giant would have run after her, but he needed to make sure none of the servants knew what he had done to your father. He knew the servants would be back soon. He knew where your father had kept all of his money and his treasures, so he stole them, and then started a fire in the house so that it would burn to the ground. The giant ran away, and no one ever found out what he had done.

"Your poor mother was alone with you—you were just a baby. She walked and walked as far away as she could get. She was very, very afraid, and so she walked quickly. She finally found the small little house where you grew up. She was so scared of the giant that she never talked of your father or what had happened.

"When your father was born, I was told to watch over him as a fairy. I had left my job for a short time when the giant was living at your house. I am terribly sorry for that. I got in trouble for that, and my powers were taken away. It was the day you met the butcher and sold your cow that I got my powers back. I am the one who made you want to take the beans for the cow.

"I made the beanstalk grow, and I am the one who made you want to climb it. The giant lives here in this country in the sky. You are the person who can make him pay for his terrible actions. It will be dangerous here, and it will be difficult, but I know you can find him and punish him.

"Everything the giant has is yours, and

it is yours to take. The only thing I ask of you is not to let your mother know I told you about your father until you see me again."

When the fairy was done talking to Jack, she disappeared. Jack was scared, but he knew he had to find the giant. He walked and walked until he found a large house. A woman opened the door, and Jack begged her for food and a place to sleep.

This surprised the woman. It was well known that her husband was a large and mean giant who spent his days hunting for people to eat. She told this to Jack, but he said he still wanted to stay. He asked her to give him a place to hide so that he could sleep and have some food. She finally agreed to take him in for one night.

As she took Jack to a hiding place, he heard terrible noises coming from the walls. These sad noises were people the giant caught and planned to eat. Jack had never been so scared in his life. He thought of his mother, and he wanted so very much to be with her. He was so foolish to climb the beanstalk! He was so foolish to come into this house!

Finally, the woman showed him to a kitchen. There was a warm fire, and she gave him a large dinner. He soon forgot how afraid he felt. But then he heard a loud knock that made the whole house shake. The giant's wife quickly helped Jack hide in the oven. She let the giant in through the kitchen door.

The giant's voice was so loud. "I smell fresh meat," he shouted.

"Foolish giant," she said. "That is just the people in your dungeon."

The giant believed her, and he stood right next to the oven. Jack was so scared that he shook. He had never been so scared in his life.

The giant sat next to the fire, and his wife made him dinner. Jack could see the giant through a small hole in the oven. He could not believe how much the giant could eat, and he thought the giant might never be done with his dinner.

Finally, the giant was done. "Bring me my hen!" the giant shouted.

His wife went to get a beautiful hen and put it on the table. Jack was very excited to see what happened next. "Lay!" yelled the giant. Jack could not believe his eyes—the hen had laid a golden egg! In fact, every time the giant said, "Lay!" the hen laid an egg of solid gold.

The giant's wife was tired, and she went to bed. The giant continued with his magic hen for hours, as Jack looked through the oven. After a time, the giant fell asleep with his hen in front of the fire. After many hours, Jack decided to sneak out of his hiding spot. As quietly as he could, he took the hen and ran away.

After a time, he came to the beanstalk. He went down the beanstalk as fast as he could, and he finally reached the bottom. He went inside his house and found his mother. His mother could not believe her eyes. She was so happy to see her son! Jack could not wait to show her what the hen could do.

"Mother," he said. "I have found something that will make us rich! I hope this makes you so happy you can forget all of the bad things that I've done. Watch what this hen can do!"

"Lay!" Jack said to the hen. Just as it did for the giant, the hen lay golden egg after golden egg. Jack and his mother sold the golden eggs, and soon they had all that they wanted.

A few months passed, and Jack and his mother had never been so happy. Jack could not forget, though, what he had heard the giant say to his wife. The giant had talked about some of his other riches. "How wonderful it would be to get those treasures," thought Jack. He knew it would upset his mother if he left again. And he also knew that it was dangerous, and probably foolish, to climb the beanstalk again. But after a time he could not help himself—he was so eager to climb it again to see what other riches he might discover. Even though his mother cried and begged him not to go, he went to climb the beanstalk a second time.

He decided to wear a disguise so that the giant's wife would not recognize him, for she would be very angry he had stolen the hen. He made the great climb into the sky, and once again, when he arrived at the top, he was hungry and tired. He rested on a rock, just as he did before. He then walked out to find the giant's house again.

He arrived at the giant's house, and the giant's wife answered the door as she did before. She did not recognize Jack in his disguise, and he asked her for food, drink, and a bed to sleep in. She told him the same thing she did last time—that her husband was a terrible and mean giant. She also told him that she had helped a poor boy once before, and that that boy had stolen the giant's greatest treasure—a hen that laid golden eggs. Jack learned that the giant was so angry he had punished his wife, for he knew it was because of his wife letting in this boy that the hen was stolen.

Jack heard her say all of this, and still he begged for food and a bed. She finally agreed. When he was done with his food and drink, she hid Jack in an old closet. The giant arrived at the same time he had before. The giant was so large that the house shook every time the giant took a step. He seated himself next to the fire, just as he had before.

"I smell fresh meat," the giant shouted again.

"That's just meat some large birds found," the wife said. "They left it on top of the house."

As the wife prepared the giant's dinner, the giant got angry and could not wait any longer. He also complained that his hen was gone. The wife quickly finished making a large pie for him to eat, and the giant ate his entire dinner in just a few seconds.

When he was done with his dinner, he said, "I need something to do. Perhaps I can count my bags of money. Or maybe my harp can make music!"

The wife brought bags of gold and

silver to him. Jack looked out from his hiding spot. The giant examined his money bags all over to be sure they were just as he had left them. He began counting his money, coin by coin by coin. As he counted, he put the coins upon the table. Jack could see the large number of coins, and he wished he could have them for his mother and himself. The giant counted each bag of money several times, and when he was done, he put the coins back in the bags and made sure to close them well.

Just as he had last time, the giant fell asleep at the table by the warm fire. The bags of money lay on the table in front of him. They were so big, and all Jack could think about was how wonderful it would be to bring these bags home for his mother and him. His mother would be so happy. Jack waited and waited. After many hours, he decided the giant must be completely asleep. He was ready to take the money bags.

Jack sneaked out of his hiding place. He put his hand on one of the bags, when he suddenly heard a noise. There was a little dog in the room! The dog had been so quiet Jack had not seen him. The dog looked right at Jack, whose hand was on the treasures, and the dog began to bark loudly, over and over and over again!

Jack was so scared he could not think. His feet could not move. He was stuck with fear. Jack thought, "Please, dog! Stop making noise!" Jack was sure he was a dead man and that the giant would wake up at any minute. But the giant continued to sleep, and after a time the dog grew tired of making noise. Jack spotted a large piece of meat and threw it to the dog, and as the dog ate the meat, Jack grabbed the dog and placed it in the closet.

Jack took both bags and ran out of the kitchen and out of the house. On his way to the beanstalk, though, he grew tired. The bags were so heavy they were very hard to carry. He was not sure he could make it, but he gathered his energy and climbed down the beanstalk to his mother.

He was so sure his mother would be waiting at the bottom for him, so happy to see her boy. But when he arrived at the bottom, he saw that the little house was empty. Where was his mother? He ran to the village and checked with the neighbors. Finally, an old woman told him his mother was in a nearby house, and that she was very, very sick.

Jack was so upset—he knew that his mother must be sick because of him. But seeing her son made his mother strong, and she got better. He gave her the bags of money, and they lived happily for three years.

Once again, Jack had trouble forgetting the beanstalk. He wanted so very much to climb it again, but he knew that was dangerous. He thought of what the fairy had told him, and he worried that the fairy would get in trouble if he did anything wrong. Still, he could not forget about the beanstalk. He made secret plans to climb it again, and for the third time, he made his climb to the top.

For the third time, he found the giant's house, and for the third time, he urged the giant's wife to take him in. She did again, and she gave him dinner again, and then put him in a hiding place again when the giant came home.

"I smell fresh meat," the giant shouted.

This time, however, instead of believing his wife's answer, the giant began looking around the room! Jack had never been so scared in his life, and he was sure he would die. The giant came closer to Jack's hiding spot in a very large pot, and Jack shook. It was Jack's lucky day—the giant did not lift the pot's lid but instead sat down by the fire.

The giant ate his entire dinner quickly, and when he was finally done, he ordered his wife to bring him his harp. She did as he asked, and brought him the most beautiful harp in the world. "Play," said the giant, and the harp began to play a wonderful song.

Jack could not believe his ears, and he knew he had to have the harp. The harp played a gentle, soft song that put the giant to sleep. Once he knew the giant was asleep, Jack came out of the pot and took the harp.

The harp, though, was under the spell of a fairy, and called out, "Giant! Giant!"

The giant woke up, and ran after Jack!

The giant had had so much to drink that he could not walk well. Jack was wide awake, and he ran as fast as he could. He was able to run faster than the giant. As Jack found the beanstalk and climbed down as fast as he could, he yelled as loudly as he could, "Bring me an ax! Bring me an ax!!" Jack was going to use the ax to cut down the beanstalk.

Jack's mother had an ax waiting, and the second Jack came down, he started to cut down the beanstalk with all the strength he had. The beanstalk started to fall over, and then broke in half. The giant, who was in the middle of climbing down, fell from the sky into the garden and died from the great fall.

Jack's mother saw the beanstalk destroyed, and she had never been so happy. The fairy appeared, and she told Jack's mother all about the giant and her husband. The fairy also made Jack promise to be as good to his mother as his father had been, and she told him this was the only way to be happy. The fairy disappeared, and Jack hugged his mother. He cried and told her he was sorry for all of the pain he had caused. She hugged him, and he promised that for the rest of his life, he would be a good son.

The History of Jack and the Giants

読みはじめる前に

The History of Jack and the Giants で使われている用語です。わからない語は巻末のワードリストで確認しましょう。

- [ ] horn
- [ ] roar
- [ ] spell
- [ ] invisible
- [ ] feast
- [ ] cave
- [ ] hurray

あらすじ

コーンウォールにジャックという賢くて勇敢な男がいました（イギリスには、ジャックという名前の人がとても多いのです）。ジャックは、町の人々を困らせる悪い巨人を退治し、「巨人殺しのジャック」と呼ばれるようになりました。

ジャックは王のため、国のため、そして自らの冒険心を満たすために巨人退治の旅にでかけます。持ち前の知恵と勇気、巨人から手に入れた魔法のアイテムを駆使して、ジャックは国中の悪い巨人たちと戦います。

Once upon a time, a rich English farmer lived in Cornwall with his son, Jack. Jack was very strong and very smart—stronger and smarter than anyone else in the village.

A large, angry giant lived just outside of Cornwall, and he would scare all of the people around him. This angry giant was especially scary because, whenever he was hungry, he would steal people's farm animals or their food. This went on for so many years that there came a time when the poor people in town had almost no food or animals left.

Jack decided he would destroy this terrible giant once and for all. He had a plan. He took a horn, a shovel, and an ax, and set off to find the giant. When he was near the giant's home, he took his tools and dug a large hole that was 22 feet deep and 22 feet wide. He covered the hole with sticks and grass so that it would be hidden. He stood right next to the hole, put the horn to his mouth, and blew hard. The horn made a loud, loud noise.

The giant woke up from his sleep, angry as could be. "You terrible boy!" shouted the giant. "You woke me up! No one does that to me! I will eat you for breakfast!"

He walked over to Jack, and as he did, he fell into the large hole. Jack looked at the giant way down deep in the hole, hit him very hard on the head, and the giant died. Jack covered the giant with dirt and filled up the hole.

Jack walked over to the giant's home and searched inside. He found many treasures. There was gold, silver, and delicious food of all kinds. Jack went

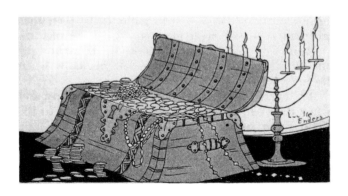

into the center of the town and said, "I have killed the giant! I have searched his house, and I have found all of these riches for us to share!" Everyone in the town jumped up and down with joy. They were so happy that the giant was dead, and they were so happy that they would have money and food again. They cried, "From now on, we will call you Jack the Giant Killer. To say thank you for all that you have done, we give you this special sword."

News of Jack the Giant Killer traveled very far. News traveled so far that even another giant, Old Blunderbore, who lived very far away, heard about it. "Who is this Jack?" said Blunderbore. "I can't believe he killed my friend. I am going to have to kill Jack."

Jack had set out looking for adventure. One day, Jack was walking near Blunderbore's woods, and he got very, very tired. He fell asleep. Blunderbore found Jack, and he knew right away that this was the boy who had killed his good friend. He picked Jack up, carried him over his shoulder, and took him to his castle.

Jack woke up as the giant walked, and he was very scared. When they arrived at the castle, Jack saw bones all around him. "These are bones of other men I have eaten," said the giant. "Tomorrow, I will eat you."

The giant locked Jack up and then left to go look for other food. Jack heard someone say, "Do what you can to get out, or else the giant will eat you up! He's gone to get his brother to help him!"

Jack was so scared. He ran to the window, and he saw two giants coming his way. Jack saw a rope, and he realized he could use the rope to catch the giants. When they opened the door, he threw the rope and caught the two giants in the rope. Once they were tied up in the rope, he got out his sword to kill them both. Once the giants were dead, he opened every door in the castle to make sure there was no one hiding that he could save.

He found three women who needed his help. "Ladies," he said. "The giant and his terrible brother are dead. You are free!"

"Thank you! What is your name?" they asked. They had very big smiles on their faces.

"I am Jack the Giant Killer," he said.

"Thank you, Jack the Giant Killer. Be safe as you continue on your adventures!"

"I will!" said Jack. He left the castle and continued on his way to Wales.

He walked, and he walked. He had no money, so he looked for a place where he could spend the night. He found a large house and decided to see if anyone was in it. He knocked, and he was very surprised to see a giant with two heads come to the gate! The giant seemed nicer than the giants Jack knew, and he invited Jack in to spend the night. He showed Jack into a bedroom.

As the giant walked away, Jack heard the giant say to himself, "You will sleep here tonight, but you will not live to see the morning light!"

The giant was not as nice as he seemed, after all! Jack was nervous, but he knew he had no time to waste. He looked around the room and tried to come up with a plan. He decided to put some wood under the bed blankets so that, when the giant came in, he would think Jack was sleeping under the blankets. Jack then hid in a dark corner of the room and waited.

Finally, in the middle of the night, the door opened. The giant came into Jack's room, stood by the bed, raised a hammer, and hit what he thought was Jack under the blankets over and over again. When the giant was sure he had killed Jack by hitting him so hard and so many times, the giant left the room.

Jack was shaking with fear, but he stayed quiet. He waited until the sun came up, so that he would be able to find his way out quietly. Very early in the morning, Jack left the giant's house and continued on his trip to Wales. As he arrived in Wales, he came upon King

Arthur's only son. King Arthur's son was traveling to find a woman to marry. He was also looking for a servant, and Jack agreed to take the job. The two of them traveled, and they gave money to those in need wherever they went. Finally, they had no money left.

"Jack, we have no money left," said the king's son. "Where should we stay tonight?"

"I can find a place," said Jack. "My uncle lives nearby. He is a giant who has three heads. We can stay with him."

"That sounds terrible!" said the king's son. "Won't he want to eat us?"

"I will take care of everything," said Jack. "Stay here and wait for me."

Jack went to the giant's house and knocked on the door. The giant answered. "I have bad news," said Jack.

"What?" asked the giant.

"The king's son is on his way, and he has an army of men who want to kill you and take all that you have."

"Oh, thank you for letting me know," said the giant. "I have a hiding spot in the basement. Lock me in there until it is safe to come out."

Jack hid the giant away. He went to get the king's son, and the two enjoyed a wonderful night in the giant's house. They stole gold and silver from the giant, too. The king's son rode away, and Jack released the giant.

"How can I ever thank you?" asked the giant.

"You are welcome," said Jack. "I don't need anything except your old sword, your coat, your hat, and your shoes."

"Sure," said the giant. "They are yours. The coat will make you invisible. The hat will make you very smart. The shoes will make you run very, very fast. I am sure that all of these things will be

very helpful to you."

Jack took them, and he left the house. He walked quickly so that he could catch up with his master.

"Thank you for finding us a place to stay," said the king's son. "Now we must go find the woman who will be my wife. She lives just through that forest." They walked and walked until they came to the house they were looking for.

"Dear lady," said Jack's master. "You shall be my wife."

"I have been waiting for you," the woman said. The woman joined the king's son and Jack, and they traveled back to King Arthur's castle where they were to be married.

They had a lovely wedding. King Arthur was so happy that Jack had helped his son find his bride, he made Jack a Knight of the Round Table.

Jack knew that he could do even more good for the king and his kingdom. "I know there are other giants in this land," he told the king. "If you give me a horse and some money, I will find them, and I will protect you and your kingdom."

"Thank you, Jack," said the king. "I will give you what you need. Now go find those giants!"

Jack took his magic hat (to make him smarter), his sword (to help him fight), his shoes (to make him run faster), and his coat (to make him invisible), and he went on his way to fight the giants. He traveled for three days until he heard a woman screaming in some woods. There he saw a beautiful woman and a knight in the hands of a great giant.

Jack quickly put on his invisible coat, and he walked right up behind the giant. He took out his sword, swung his sword, and he tried to kill the giant. The giant was so big, however, that Jack could only cut the giant's legs. The giant was not dead, but he did fall to the ground. As the giant fell, the knight and the lady were able to escape the giant's hands.

"You are terrible!" Jack yelled at the giant. "I am Jack the Giant Killer! And you will pay for hurting this knight and this woman!" Jack put his sword into the giant's body, and he ran to catch up with the knight and the lady.

"We cannot thank you enough," said the knight and the lady. "Please come to our house so that we can give you a gift to say thank you."

"That is very nice of you," said Jack. "But I must find where this giant lived. I cannot rest until I am sure there are no other giants that could hurt you at his house."

"But you might get hurt!" said the knight. "I can't let you do that."

"I must do this," said Jack. "It is my job to make sure there are no giants left anywhere in this kingdom. Once I am certain that there are no more giants, I will come back and visit you both."

So Jack got back on his horse and went to look for the giant's house. He had ridden one mile when he came to a cave and saw a terrible, scary giant. Jack got off his horse and put on his coat to make him invisible. He walked very quietly up to the giant from behind. He decided to use his sword again, and he took a big swing at the giant. He missed the giant's heart, but he cut off the giant's nose.

The giant cried out in terrible pain. "Ow!" the giant yelled. "Who did that?" he roared.

Jack danced around the giant, deciding what to do next, as the giant continued to scream in pain. Jack swung his sword at the giant again, and the giant danced about with the sword still stuck in his body. "Ow! Who is doing this?" he cried. "I don't see anyone there!"

Eventually, the pain became too great, and the giant fell down dead. Jack wanted King Arthur to know for sure that Jack had protected the kingdom, so he cut off the giant's head and sent it on his horse to the King.

With the giant gone, Jack decided to go inside the giant's cave to look for treasures. He entered the cave carefully. He walked and walked, looking around him as he went deeper and deeper into the cave. Eventually, he came to the cave's end, where he saw a large table and a large pot over a burning fire. There was also a large gate. Jack walked up to the gate and looked through it.

"Who's there?" voices cried from behind the gate. "Is there someone here to save us?"

"Who are you?" Jack asked. "And why are you behind this gate?"

"The terrible giant grabbed us and brought us here. He has kept us here to fatten us up until he is ready to eat us. Just recently, he took three of our friends and ate them for dinner."

"I don't think you need to worry about that happening to you," said Jack.

"Why not?" said the prisoners. "We

are so scared. Are you going to hurt us?"

"Oh no! I killed the giant with my own sword," said Jack. "I even sent his head to King Arthur so that he knows I have saved his kingdom from this terrible giant."

Jack unlocked the gate, and the prisoners came forward. "Oh wonderful day!" they cried out. "You have saved us! You have saved us!"

They all sat around the giant's table, happy to be free of the terrible giant at last. They found some food—meat, bread, and wine—and had a feast.

When they were finished with their wonderful meal, they were happy to be full and safe. They looked around the cave and found large amounts of gold and silver. Jack divided up the treasure equally. They slept soundly in the cave, and the next morning, they set out to go back to their homes.

Jack remembered his promise to the knight—that he would return to the knight and his lady after his work was done. He got on his horse and traveled back to the knight's house. He arrived around lunchtime.

"Thank goodness you are safe!" cried the knight. "We shall celebrate your return with a feast!"

The feast lasted for many days, and people came from all over to celebrate. "Hurray for Jack the Giant Killer!"

people cried out. As a gift to show how much they appreciated what Jack had done, the knight gave Jack a gold ring.

Some of the prisoners' fathers came to Jack to thank him. "Thank you, Jack the Giant Killer, for saving our children!" Jack smiled.

As everyone celebrated, a dark cloud appeared in the sky. Everyone looked up. They were scared and wondered what might happen, when all of a sudden a messenger appeared from the sky. "I come with a message from Thunderdel, a giant with two heads. Thunderdel lives on this island, and he is coming to get you, Jack, for you have killed Thunderdel's friends and family. He is only one mile away. He will get you soon!"

"I am not scared!" Jack said. "He can come for me! When he arrives, I will be ready!"

The town people cheered and cried. "Hurray for Jack the Giant Killer!"

Jack turned to the people. "You, my people, can watch. I will destroy that giant, and I will save us all!"

The townspeople came forward to wish Jack good luck. "We know you can do it!" they told Jack. They knew that if anyone could fight this giant, it was Jack. Jack would save them.

Jack had a plan. The knight's house was on a small island. Jack knew that the only way off the island was by a small bridge. Jack asked two men for help, and they cut the bridge just enough to weaken it. Jack knew that if someone as large and heavy as a giant tried to cross it, the bridge would break in half. Jack put on his invisible coat so that he could surprise the giant. He held up his sword and waited. He was ready to fight.

Soon enough, Jack saw the giant in the distance coming toward the knight's house. The giant could not see Jack, but he could feel the presence of danger all around him. "Fe, fi, fo, fum!" the giant cried. "I smell the blood of an Englishman. He may be alive, he may be dead. I'll use his bones to make my bread."

"Oh, really?" said Jack. The giant looked all around to see where this voice was coming from. "You are a terrible giant, for sure," said Jack. "But I think I will do to you what I have done to all of your friends and family."

"Who's there?" said the giant. "Are you the giant killer? If you are, I will eat you, right down to the bones. And I will use your bones to make bread!" roared the giant.

"Well, first you'll have to catch me," said Jack. He threw off his coat so that the giant could see him, and he ran away. The giant ran after him, roaring. The ground shook. Jack ran around and around the knight's house so that the gentlemen and ladies who were all watching could get a good look at the battle. Every time it seemed like the giant could catch up to Jack, Jack used his special shoes to run faster and faster. There was no way the giant could catch up to Jack—Jack was as fast as the wind. When Jack was sure the giant was behind him, Jack ran over the bridge. Jack crossed the bridge, and he turned to look at the giant coming his way. As the giant ran over the bridge, the bridge shook, and it broke in two. The giant tumbled into the water below.

Jack laughed from the land above. "Ha, ha, ha, ha! I got you!" Jack cried.

The giant watched Jack cry out with

laughter, and this made the giant only more and more angry. The giant was trying to get out of the water, but he

could not swim well. Jack watched the giant, and as the giant got more tired, Jack threw his sword at the giant. The sword hit the giant in his heart, killing him immediately. As he now had done many times before, Jack cut off the giant's head and sent it by horse to King Arthur.

"Thank goodness for Jack the Giant Killer!" cheered all of the ladies and gentlemen. "Let's continue this feast! Let us continue to celebrate!"

Days later, Jack grew tired of the celebration. He wanted new adventures. He decided to move on, traveling by horse to find something exciting and new to do. He came upon a small house late one night. The house was at the bottom of a mountain. Jack knocked on the door.

An old man with white hair answered the door.

"Sir," said Jack. "Do you have a place where I might stay? I need a place to sleep tonight, and I need some food for I am very hungry."

"Of course," said the old man. "Please, come in. You may stay in my house, and I will feed you."

Jack went into the man's warm little house. "I am guessing you are Jack the Giant Killer," said the old man. "On top of the mountain here, we have a terrible, terrible giant named Galligantus. He is evil, and he has magic powers. He turns anyone who he finds into other shapes and objects. He even took the duke's daughter, and he turned her into a deer. Many people have tried to break the spell and have tried to kill the giant. But the duke's daughter has remained a deer for years and years. I hope that with your invisible coat, you might be able to get into the giant's castle and read the spell that can turn her back into a lady."

"This is just the adventure I have been looking for," said Jack. "Of course I will try. I will head up the mountain in the morning, and I will free the duke's daughter from this terrible spell. She will no longer be a deer."

The two men ate and went to bed. In the morning, Jack got up early. He put on his special magical cap, shoes, and coat, and he prepared his sword.

He climbed and climbed until he got to the top of the mountain. He came upon the castle and saw at the gates a golden trumpet. The trumpet read, "He who blows this trumpet shall break the giant's spell."

Of course, Jack quickly blew the trumpet. The castle began to crumble, and Jack heard a giant's roar. Jack saw the giant, and the giant knew Jack had broken the spell, and that he would soon die.

Jack ran up to the giant, took his sword, and cut off the giant's head. The spell was broken, and all kinds of birds, animals, and creatures were turned back into people. Even the castle itself disappeared. The people who were freed from the spell cheered and yelled, "Hurray! You saved us! Thank you for saving us!" Once again, Jack took the head of the giant, and send it by horse to King Arthur.

Jack felt that this was his final act against the giants, and he set off to return to King Arthur. As he traveled, people came forward to thank Jack for all of his good deeds. "You have saved us!" they cried. Everyone had lived in fear of the giants, and they could now relax and rejoice.

Finally, Jack arrived at King Arthur's

castle. "Thank you, Jack!" said King Arthur. "We all appreciate what you have done for us. To show you how very much I thank you, I give you my daughter to marry. There is no man as brave as you, and no man as good as you. I can think of no one else I would like to make my son."

Jack smiled and took the King's daughter's hand. They had a beautiful wedding, and the kingdom was filled with happiness and laughter. Jack and King Arthur's daughter lived happily ever after.

Word List

- 本文で使われている全ての語を掲載しています（LEVEL 1, 2）。ただし、LEVEL 3以上は、中学校レベルの語を含みません。
- 語形が規則変化する語の見出しは原形で示しています。不規則変化語は本文中で使われている形になっています。
- 一般的な意味を紹介していますので、一部の語で本文で実際に使われている品詞や意味と合っていないことがあります。
- 品詞は以下のように示しています。

名 名詞	代 代名詞	形 形容詞	副 副詞	動 動詞	助 助動詞
前 前置詞	接 接続詞	間 間投詞	冠 冠詞	略 略語	俗 俗語
頭 接頭語	尾 接尾語	号 記号	関 関係代名詞		

A

- **a** 冠 ①1つの, 1人の, ある ②~につき
- **able to** 形《be-》（人が）~することができる
- **about** 副 まわりに, あたりを 前 ①~について ②~のまわりに[の]
- **above** 副 上に
- **act** 名 行為, 行い
- **action** 名 行為
- **adventure** 名 冒険
- **afraid** 形 恐れて, こわがって
- **after** 前 ①~の後に[で], ~の次に ②《前後に名詞がきて》次々に~, 何度も~《反復・継続を表す》 副 後に[で] 接（~した）後に[で] **after all** 結局のところ **ever after** その後ずっと **happily ever after** それからずっと幸せに暮らしましたとさ **one after another** 次々に, 1つ[人]ずつ
- **again** 副 再び, もう一度 **over and over again** 何度も繰り返して
- **against** 前 ~に対して
- **age** 名 年齢
- **agree** 動 同意する, 意見が一致する **agree on** ~について合意する
- **air** 名《the-》空中
- **alive** 形 生きている
- **all** 形 すべての, ~中 代 全部, すべて（のもの[人]）名 全体 副 まったく, すっかり **after all** 結局のところ **all kinds of** さまざまな, あらゆる種類の **all of a sudden** 突然, 前触れもなしに **all over** ~中で, 全体にわたって, ~の至る所で **all year** 一年中, 一年を通して **once and for all** きっぱりと
- **almost** 副 ほとんど
- **alone** 形 ただひとりの 副 ひとりで, ~だけで
- **along** 前 ~に沿って, 前へ **come along** やって来る, 現れる **send ~ along** ~を送り届ける
- **already** 副 すでに, もう
- **also** 副 ~も（また）, ~も同様に 接 その上, さらに
- **always** 副 いつも, 常に
- **am** 動 ~である, (~に)いる[ある]《主語がIのときのbeの現在形》
- **amount** 名 量, 額
- **an** 冠 ①1つの, 1人の, ある ②~につき
- **and** 接 ①そして, ~と… ②《同じ語を結んで》ますます ③《結果を表

100

Word List

- **and** 《〜して》それで, だから **and so** そこで, それだから
- **angry** 形 怒って, 腹を立てて **get angry** 腹を立てる
- **animal** 名 動物
- **another** 形 ①もう1つ[1人]の ②別の 代 ①もう1つ[1人] ②別のもの **one after another** 次々に, 1つ[1人]ずつ
- **answer** 動 答える, 応じる 名 答え, 返事
- **any** 形 ①《否定文で》何も, 少しも（〜ない）②《肯定文で》どの〜も **not〜any longer** もはや〜でない[〜しない]
- **anyone** 代 ①《疑問文・条件節で》誰か ②《否定文で》誰も（〜ない）③《肯定文で》誰でも
- **anything** 代 ①《疑問文で》何か, どれでも ②《否定文で》何も, どれも（〜ない）③《肯定文で》何でも, どれでも
- **anyway** 副 いずれにせよ, ともかく
- **anywhere** 副 どこにも
- **appear** 動 現れる
- **apple** 名 リンゴ
- **appreciate** 動 ありがたく思う, 感謝する
- **are** 動 〜である,（〜に）いる[ある] 《主語がyou, we, theyまたは複数名詞のときのbeの現在形》
- **army** 名 部隊, 集団
- **around** 副 ①まわりに, あちこちに ②およそ, 約 前 〜のまわりに, 〜のあちこちに
- **arrive** 動 到着する, 到達する **arrive at** 〜に着く **arrive in** 〜に着く
- **as** 接 ①《as 〜 asの形で》…と同じくらい〜 ②〜のとおりに, 〜のように ③〜しながら, 〜しているときに ④〜するにつれて, 〜にしたがって ⑤〜なので ⑥〜だけれども ⑦〜する限りでは 前 ①〜として（の）②〜の時 副 同じくらい 代 ①〜のような ②〜だが **as a result** その結果（として）**as 〜 as one can** できる限り〜 **just as** 〜と全く同じように, 〜のとおりに
- **ask** 動 ①尋ねる, 聞く ②頼む, 求める **ask if one could** 〜してもいいかと聞く **ask someone if** 〜かどうかを（人）にたずねる
- **asleep** 形 眠って（いる状態の）副 眠って, 休止して **fall asleep** 眠り込む, 寝入る
- **at** 前 ①《場所・時》〜に[で] ②《目標・方向》〜に[を], 〜に向かって ③《原因・理由》〜を見て[聞いて・知って] ④〜に従事して, 〜の状態で
- **ate** 動 eat（食べる）の過去
- **awake** 形 目が覚めて
- **away** 副 離れて, 遠くに, 去って, わきに 形 離れた **far away** 遠く離れて **right away** すぐに
- **ax** 名 おの

B

- **baby** 名 赤ん坊
- **back** 名 背中, 後ろ 副 ①戻って ②後ろへ[に] 形 裏の, 後ろの **back and forth** 行きつ戻りつ
- **bad** 形 ①悪い ②気の毒な, 後悔している **feel bad** 後悔する
- **bag** 名 袋, かばん
- **baptize** 動 洗礼を施す
- **bark** 動 ほえる
- **basement** 名 地下(室)
- **battle** 名 戦闘, 戦い
- **be** 動 〜である,（〜に）いる[ある], 〜となる 助 ①《現在分詞とともに用いて》〜している ②《過去分詞とともに用いて》〜される, 〜されている
- **bean** 名 豆

English Folk Tales

- **beanstalk** 名豆の茎
- **beat** 動打つ
- **beautiful** 形美しい,すばらしい
- **became** 動 become (なる) の過去
- **because** 接 (なぜなら) 〜だから,〜という理由[原因]で **because of** 〜のために,〜の理由で
- **bed** 名ベッド,寝所 **go to bed** 床につく,寝る **go to bed hungry** 空腹のまま寝る
- **bedroom** 名寝室
- **been** 動 be (〜である) の過去分詞 助 be (〜している・〜される) の過去分詞
- **before** 前〜の前に[で],〜より以前に 接〜する前に 副以前に
- **beg** 動懇願する,乞い願う
- **began** 動 begin (始まる) の過去
- **begin** 動始まる[始める],起こる
- **beginning** 動 begin (始まる) の現在分詞 名初め,始まり
- **behind** 前〜の後ろに,〜の背後に 副後ろに,背後に
- **being** 動 be (〜である) の現在分詞
- **believe** 動信じる,信じている,(〜と) 思う,考える
- **below** 副下に[へ]
- **better** 形 ①よりよい ②(人が) 回復して 副 ①よりよく,より上手に ②〜したほうがいい **get better** (病気などが) 良くなる **know better than to** 〜するほどばかではない,〜しないほうがいいと分かっている
- **between A and B** AとBの間
- **big** 形大きい,強力な
- **bird** 名鳥
- **blanket** 名毛布
- **blew** 動 blow (吹く) の過去
- **blood** 名血
- **blow** 動 ①息を吹く ②吹奏する **blow down** 吹き倒す

- **Blunderbore** 名ブランダーボア《人名》
- **boat** 名ボート,小舟
- **body** 名体,胴体
- **bone** 名骨
- **born** 動《be-》生まれる
- **both** 形両方の,2つとも 副《both 〜 and の形で》〜も…も両方とも 代両方,両者
- **bottom** 名下部,ふもと
- **bought** 動 buy (買う) の過去,過去分詞
- **boy** 名少年,男の子
- **brave** 形勇敢な
- **bread** 名パン
- **break** 動 ①壊す,折る ②中断する,遮断する **break in two** 二つに折れる
- **breakfast** 名朝食
- **brick** 名レンガ 形レンガ造りの
- **bride** 名花嫁
- **bridge** 名橋
- **bright** 形輝いている,鮮明な
- **bring** 動 ①持ってくる,連れてくる ②もたらす,生じる **bring〜home** 〜を家に持ってくる
- **broke** 動 break (壊す) の過去
- **broken** 動 break (壊す) の過去分詞
- **brother** 名 ①兄弟 ②仲間
- **brought** 動 bring (持ってくる) の過去,過去分詞
- **build** 動建てる
- **built** 動 build (建てる) の過去,過去分詞
- **bundle** 名束
- **burn** 動燃える,燃やす **burn to the ground** 全焼する
- **but** 接 ①でも,しかし ②〜を除いて 前〜を除いて,〜のほかは 副ただ,のみ,ほんの **not〜but** 〜ではな

- **butcher** 名 肉屋
- **butter maker** バター製造機
- **buy** 動 買う
- **by** 前 ①《位置》〜のそばに[で] ②《手段・方法・行為者・基準》〜によって,〜で ③《期限》〜までには ④《通過・経由》〜を経由して,〜を通って 副 そばに,通り過ぎて

C

- **call** 動 呼ぶ,叫ぶ **call in** 〜を呼ぶ **call out** 叫ぶ
- **came** 動 come(来る)の過去
- **can** 動 ①〜できる ②〜してもよい ③〜でありうる ④《否定文で》〜のはずがない **as 〜 as one can** できる限り〜 **cannot〜 enough** いくら〜してもしたりない
- **cane** 名 (籐製の)杖
- **cap** 名 (縁なしの)帽子
- **care** 名 心配,世話 動《通例否定文・疑問文で》気にする,心配する **take care of** 〜の世話をする,〜の面倒を見る
- **carefully** 副 注意深く
- **carry** 動 運ぶ,持ち歩く
- **castle** 名 城,大邸宅
- **catch** 動 ①つかまえる ②追いつく **catch up to** 〜に追いつく
- **caught** 動 catch(つかまえる)の過去,過去分詞
- **cause** 動 (〜の)原因となる,引き起こす
- **cave** 名 洞穴,洞窟
- **celebrate** 動 祝う,祝典を開く
- **celebration** 名 祝賀会
- **center** 名 中心,中央
- **certain** 形 (人が)確信した
- **certainly** 副 必ず,確実に
- **change** 動 変える
- **check** 動 確認する,チェックする
- **cheer** 動 かっさいを送る
- **cheese** 名 チーズ
- **child** 名 子ども
- **children** 名 child(子ども)の複数
- **chimney** 名 煙突
- **chinny-chin-chin** 名 あご(chin のふざけた言い方) **Not by the hair of my chinny-chin-chin**(あごひげにかけて)絶対やだね《言葉遊び的表現》
- **Christabel** 名 クリスタベル《人名》
- **circle** 名 円,輪 **in a circle** 輪になって
- **city** 名 (大聖堂のある)町,市
- **climb** 動 登る,徐々に上がる **climb down** 〜からはい降りる **make a climb into** 〜に上がっていく
- **close** 形 近い 動 閉める **take a closer look** もう少し近くで見る
- **closely** 副 接近して,詳しく
- **closet** 名 戸棚,物置
- **clothes** 名 衣服
- **cloud** 名 雲
- **coat** 名 外套,コート
- **coin** 名 硬貨,コイン
- **color** 名 色
- **come** 動 ①来る,行く,現れる ②(出来事が)起こる,生じる ③〜になる ④come の過去分詞 **come along** やって来る,現れる **come and 〜** 〜しに行く **come back** 戻る **come down** 下りて来る **come for** 〜に向かってくる **come forward** 前に進み出る **come in** 中にはいる **come into** 〜に入ってくる **come out** 外に出る **come out of** 〜から出てくる **come over to** 〜にやって来る **come up** 昇る,現れる **come up with** 〜を考え出す,見つけ出す **come upon** 〜に偶然

- □ **complain** 動不平を言う, ぶつぶつ言う
- □ **completely** 副完全に, すっかり
- □ **continue** 動続く, 続ける, (中断後)再開する, (ある方向に)移動していく continue on one's way 歩き続ける
- □ **cook** 動料理する
- □ **corner** 名角, すみ
- □ **Cornwall** 名コーンウォール《地名》
- □ **could** 助①can (〜できる)の過去②《控え目な推量・可能性・願望などを表す》How could 〜? 何だって〜なんてことがありえようか? ask if one could 〜してもいいかと聞く could have done 〜だったかもしれない《仮定法》
- □ **count** 動数える count out loud 声に出して数える
- □ **country** 名国, 地域
- □ **course** 熟《of-》もちろん, 当然
- □ **cover** 動覆う, 包む, 隠す
- □ **cow** 名雌牛, 乳牛
- □ **creature** 名生物
- □ **cross** 動横切る, 渡る
- □ **crumble** 動崩れる
- □ **cry** 動泣く, 叫ぶ, 大声を出す cry out 叫ぶ
- □ **cut** 動①切る, 切断する ②cutの過去, 過去分詞 cut down 切り倒す, 打ちのめす cut off 切断する cut 〜 up 〜を切り刻む

D

- □ **dance** 動小刻みに動く, 飛び跳ねる dance about 跳ね回る
- □ **danger** 名危険, 脅威
- □ **dangerous** 形危険な
- □ **dark** 形暗い, 黒い
- □ **daughter** 名娘
- □ **day** 名日 every single day 一日も欠かさずに one day ある日 to this day 今日に至るまで
- □ **dead** 形死んでいる 副完全に
- □ **dear** 形親愛なる, 大事な 名ねえ, あなた《呼びかけ》
- □ **death** 名死
- □ **decide** 動決定[決意]する, (〜しようと)決める, 判決を下す decide to do 〜することに決める
- □ **deed** 名行為, 行動
- □ **deep** 形深い, 深さ〜の
- □ **deer** 名シカ(鹿)
- □ **definitely** 副間違いなく
- □ **delicious** 形おいしい, うまい
- □ **destroy** 動破壊する, 殺す
- □ **did** 動 do (〜をする)の過去 助 doの過去
- □ **die** 動死ぬ
- □ **different** 形違った, 別の
- □ **difficult** 形困難な
- □ **dig** 動掘る
- □ **dinner** 名夕食
- □ **dirt** 名泥, 土
- □ **disappear** 動姿を消す, なくなる
- □ **discover** 動発見する
- □ **disguise** 名変装(すること)
- □ **distance** 名遠方 in the distance 遠方に
- □ **divide up** 分ける
- □ **do** 助①《ほかの動詞とともに用いて現在形の否定文・疑問文をつくる》②《同じ動詞を繰り返す代わりに用いる》③《動詞を強調するのに用いる》動〜をする do good for 〜のためになることをする do with 〜を処理する
- □ **does** 動 do (〜をする)の3人称単数現在 助 doの3人称単数現在

出あう, 出くわす

Word List

- □ **dog** 名犬
- □ **done** 動 do（〜をする）の過去分詞
- □ **door** 名扉、ドア
- □ **down** 副 ①下へ、降りて、低くなって ②倒れて 前 〜の下方へ、〜を下って 形 下方の、下りの **right down to** 〜まで徹底的に
- □ **dress** 名礼装、ドレス
- □ **drink** 動飲む、飲酒する 名飲み物、酒
- □ **drop** 動落とす
- □ **drown** 動おぼれる、溺死する[させる]
- □ **dug** 動 dig（掘る）の過去、過去分詞
- □ **duke** 名公爵
- □ **dungeon** 名地下牢
- □ **during** 前 〜の間（ずっと）

E

- □ **each** 形それぞれの、各自の 副それぞれに **each other** お互いに
- □ **eager** 形《be-to》しきりに〜したがっている
- □ **ear** 名耳、聴覚
- □ **early** 形（時間や時期が）早い 副早く、早めに
- □ **eat** 動食べる、食事する **eat 〜 up** 〜を平らげる
- □ **eaten** 動 eat（食べる）の過去分詞
- □ **edge** 名端、縁
- □ **eel** 名ウナギ（鰻）
- □ **egg** 名卵
- □ **else** 副 ①そのほかに[の]、代わりに ②さもないと **no one else** 他の誰一人として〜しない **or else** さもないと
- □ **empty** 動空にする
- □ **end** 名果て、端
- □ **energy** 名力、精力
- □ **English** 形英国（人）の
- □ **Englishman** 名イングランド人、イギリス人
- □ **enjoy** 動楽しむ
- □ **enough** 形十分な、（〜するに）足る 副（〜できる）だけ、十分に、まったく **cannot 〜 enough** いくら〜してもしたりない **enough to do** 〜するのに十分な **sure enough** 確かに
- □ **enter** 動入る
- □ **entire** 形全部の
- □ **equally** 副等しく、平等に
- □ **escape** 動逃げる
- □ **especially** 副特別に、とりわけ
- □ **even** 副《強意》〜でさえも、〜ですら、いっそう、さらに **even though** 〜にもかかわらず
- □ **eventually** 副結局は
- □ **ever** 副 ①いつまでも ②《強意》いったい ③決して（〜ない） **ever after** その後ずっと **happily ever after** それからずっと幸せに暮らしましたとさ
- □ **every** 形 ①どの〜も、すべての、あらゆる ②毎〜、〜ごとの **every single day** 一日も欠かさずに **every time** 〜するときはいつも、〜のたびに
- □ **everyone** 代誰でも、皆
- □ **everything** 代すべてのこと[もの]、何でも、何もかも **mean everything to** 〜にとって重要な
- □ **evil** 形邪悪な、悪意のある
- □ **examine** 動（詳細に）調べる
- □ **except** 前 〜を除いて、〜のほかは
- □ **excited** 形興奮した、わくわくした **be excited to** 大喜びで〜する
- □ **exciting** 形興奮させる、わくわくさせる
- □ **expect** 動予期[予測]する
- □ **eye** 名目、視力

F

- **face** 名顔
- **fact** 名事実　in fact つまり
- **fair** 名市場, 縁日
- **fairy** 名妖精
- **fall** 動①落ちる, 倒れる ②(ある状態に)急に陥る 名落下, 墜落　fall asleep 眠り込む, 寝入る　fall down くずれる, 倒れる　fall out 落ちる, 飛び出す　fall over 倒れる　fall to the ground 転ぶ
- **family** 名家族
- **far** 副遠くに, はるかに, 離れて 形遠い, 向こうの　far away 遠く離れて
- **farm** 名農場, 飼育所
- **farmer** 名農場経営者
- **farther** 副さらに先に 形もっと向こうの
- **fast** 形(速度が)速い 副速く
- **father** 名父親
- **fatten** 動太らせる
- **fe, fi, fo, fum** フィー・ファイ・フォ・ファン《鼻歌》
- **fear** 名恐れ, 不安　in fear ビクビクして　with fear 怖がって
- **feast** 名饗宴, ごちそう 動大いに楽しむ　feast on ～を大いに楽しむ
- **feed** 動食物を与える
- **feel** 動感じる, (～と)思う　feel bad 後悔する　feel like ～のような感じがする
- **feet** 名①foot(足)の複数 ②フィート《長さの単位。約30cm》
- **fell** 動fall(落ちる)の過去
- **felt** 動feel(感じる)の過去, 過去分詞
- **few** 形《a ～》少しの
- **field** 名田畑
- **fifth** 形第5番目の
- **fight** 動(～と)戦う, 争う
- **fill** 動満ちる, 満たす《be -ed with ～》～でいっぱいである　fill up (穴・すき間を)いっぱいに満たす, 詰める
- **final** 形最後の, 決定的な
- **finally** 副最後に, ついに, 結局
- **find** 動①見つける ②(～と)わかる, 気づく, ～と考える ③得る　find one's way out 解決策を見いだす　find out 気がつく, 知る
- **finish** 動終わる, 終える　finish doing ～するのを終える
- **fire** 名火, 炎　start a fire 火をつける
- **fireplace** 名暖炉
- **first** 形第一の, 最初の 副第一に, 最初に　for the first time in one's life 生まれて初めて
- **fish** 名魚
- **fishing** 名釣り 形釣りの
- **five** 名5(の数字)
- **flew** 動fly(飛ぶ)の過去
- **fly** 動飛ぶ　fly away 飛び去る
- **food** 名食物
- **fool** 名ばか者
- **foolish** 形おろかな, ばかばかしい
- **for** 前①《目的・原因・対象》～にとって, ～のために[の], ～に対して ②《期間》～間 ③《代理》～の代わりに ④《方向》～へ(向かって) 接というわけは～, なぜなら～, だから
- **forest** 名森林
- **forget** 動忘れる
- **forgot** 動forget(忘れる)の過去, 過去分詞
- **forth** 副前へ　back and forth 行きつ戻りつ
- **forward** 副前方に, 進んで　come forward 前に進み出る
- **fought** 動fight(戦う)の過去, 過去分詞

Word List

- **found** 動 find（見つける）の過去, 過去分詞
- **four** 名 4（の数字）
- **fourth** 形 第4番目の
- **free** 形 自由な, 開放された 動 自由にする, 解放する
- **fresh** 形 新鮮な
- **Friday** 名 金曜日 Good Friday 聖金曜日《キリストの受難記念日》
- **friend** 名 友だち, 仲間
- **from** 前 ①《出身・出発点・時間・順序・原料》～から ②《原因・理由》～がもとで from now on 今後
- **front** 名 正面, 前 in front of ～の前に, ～の正面に
- **full** 形 満腹の

G

- **Galligantus** 名 ガリガンタス《人名》
- **garden** 名 庭, 庭園
- **gate** 名 門扉, 入り口
- **gather** 動 集める
- **gave** 動 give（与える）の過去
- **gentle** 形 優しい
- **gentleman** 名 紳士
- **gentlemen** 名 gentleman（紳士）の複数
- **get** 動 ①得る, 手に入れる ②（ある状態に）なる, いたる ③わかる, 理解する ④～させる, ～を（…の状態に）する ⑤（ある場所に）達する, 着く ⑥やっつける, 殺す get a good look ～をよく見る get angry 腹を立てる get back 戻る, 帰る get～back ～を取り戻す get better（病気が）良くなる get in trouble 厄介ごとに巻き込まれる, 災難に見舞われる get into ～に入り込む get off（～から）降りる get on（乗り物などに）乗る get out ①出て行く, 逃げ出す ②取り出す, 抜き出す get out of ～から外へ出る［抜け出る］ get someone to do（人）に～させる［してもらう］ get to ～に達する［到着する］ get up 起床する
- **giant** 名 巨人
- **gift** 名 贈り物
- **Gilbert** 名 ギルバート《人名》
- **give** 動 与える, 贈る
- **glad** 形 うれしい
- **go** 動 ①行く, 出かける ②動く ③進む, 経過する, いたる ④（ある状態に）なる be going to ～するつもりである go back to ～に帰る［戻る］ go doing ～をしに行く go down 下に降りる go home 帰宅する go into ～に入る go on 進み続ける, 起こる go on one's way 道を進む go out 出て行く go over ～をおおう go to bed 床につく, 寝る go to bed hungry 空腹のまま寝る
- **god** 名 神 thank god ありがたい
- **godfather** 名 名付け親（男性の）
- **godmother** 名 名付け親（女性の）
- **godparent** 名《-s》名付け親
- **gold** 名 金, 金貨 形 金の, 金製の
- **golden** 形 金色の, 金の
- **gone** 動 go（行く）の過去分詞 形 去った
- **good** 形 よい, 善良な do good for ～のためになることをする get a good look ～をよく見る Good Friday 聖金曜日《キリストの受難記念日》
- **goodness** 名 よいこと thank goodness ありがたい, よかった
- **got** 動 get（得る）の過去, 過去分詞
- **Gotham** 名 ゴッサム《地名》
- **grab** 動 ひっつかむ
- **grass** 名 草
- **great** 形 ①大きい,（量や程度が）たいへんな, すばらしい ②えらい

English Folk Tales

- **green** 形 緑色の, 青々とした
- **grew** 動 grow (成長する) の過去
- **ground** 名 地面, 土, 土地 **burn to the ground** 全焼する **fall to the ground** 転ぶ **to the ground** 徹底的に
- **group** 名 集団, 群
- **grow** 動 ①成長する, 育つ ②(次第に~に)なる **grow up** 成長する
- **guess** 動 推測する, (~と)思う **guess what** 一体何なのか当ててみる

H

- **ha** 間 は, ほう《驚き・喜び・笑い声などを表す》
- **had** 動 have (持つ) の過去, 過去分詞 助 have の過去《過去完了の文をつくる》
- **hair** 名 髪, 毛 **Not by the hair of my chinny-chin-chin** あごひげにかけて絶対やだね《言葉遊び的表現》
- **half** 名 半分
- **hammer** 名 ハンマー, 金づち
- **hand** 名 手
- **happen** 動 (出来事が) 起こる, 生じる
- **happily** 副 幸福に, 楽しく **happily ever after** それからずっと幸せに暮らしましたとさ
- **happiness** 名 幸せ, 喜び
- **happy** 形 幸せな, うれしい, 満足して **be happy to do** ~してうれしい
- **hard** 形 厳しい, きつい 副 一生懸命に, 激しく **hard to** ~し難い
- **harp** 名 ハープ《楽器》
- **has** 動 have (持つ) の3人称単数現在 助 have の3人称単数現在《現在完了の文をつくる》
- **hat** 名 (縁のある) 帽子

- **have** 動 ①持つ, 持っている, 抱く ②(~が)ある, いる ③食べる, 飲む ④経験する, (病気に)かかる ⑤催す, 開く ⑥(人に)~させる 助《〈have +過去分詞〉の形で現在完了の文をつくる》~した, ~したことがある, ずっと~している **could have done** ~だったかもしれない《仮定法》**have no time to do** ~する時間がない **have trouble** ~するのに苦労する
- **he** 代 彼は[が]
- **head** 名 ①頭 ②長, 指導者 動 向かう **head of** ~の長
- **hear** 動 聞く, 耳にする **hear about** ~について聞く **hear from** ~から連絡をもらう
- **heard** 動 hear (聞く) の過去, 過去分詞
- **heart** 名 心臓, 胸
- **heavy** 形 重い
- **held** 動 hold (つかむ) の過去, 過去分詞
- **hello** 間 こんにちは, やあ
- **help** 動 助ける, 手伝う 名 助け, 手伝い **can not help oneself** 自分を抑えられない
- **helpful** 形 役に立つ
- **hen** 名 雌鳥
- **her** 代 ①彼女を[に] ②彼女の
- **here** 副 ここに[で] 名 ここ
- **herself** 代 彼女自身
- **hid** 動 hide (隠れる) の過去, 過去分詞
- **hidden** 動 hide (隠れる) の過去分詞
- **hide** 動 隠れる, 隠す **hide ~ away** ~を隠す **hiding spot [place]** 隠れ家[場所]
- **high** 形 高い
- **hill** 名 丘
- **him** 代 彼を[に]
- **himself** 代 彼自身

Word List

- **his** 代 ①彼の ②彼のもの
- **history** 名 過去のこと, 前歴
- **hit** 動 ①打つ, なぐる ②hitの過去, 過去分詞
- **hold** 動 つかむ, ~を手に持つ hold up ~を持ち上げる
- **hole** 名 穴, すき間
- **home** 名 家, 故郷 bring~home ~を家に持ってくる go home 帰宅する
- **hope** 動 望む, (~であるようにと)思う
- **horn** 名 角笛
- **horse** 名 馬
- **hot** 形 熱い
- **hour** 名 1時間, 時間
- **house** 名 家, 建物, 小屋
- **how** 副 ①どうやって, どれくらい, どんなふうに ②なんて(~だろう) ③《関係副詞》~する方法 How could ~? 何だって~なんてことがありえようか? no matter how どんなに~であろうとも
- **however** 接 けれども, だが
- **hug** 動 しっかりと抱き締める
- **Humphrey** 名 ハンフリー《人名》
- **hundred** 名 100(の数字) hundreds of 何百もの~
- **hungry** 形 空腹の, 飢えた go to bed hungry 空腹のまま寝る
- **hunt** 動 狩りをする
- **hurray** 間 ばんざい, フレー《歓喜・賞賛・激励などを表す声》
- **hurt** 動 傷つける, 害する
- **husband** 名 夫

I

- **I** 代 私は[が]
- **idea** 名 考え, 計画
- **if** 接 もし~ならば, たとえ~でも, ~かどうか ask if one could ~してもいいかと聞く ask someone if ~かどうかを(人)にたずねる not sure if ~かどうかわからない see if ~かどうかを確かめる wonder if ~ではないかと思う
- **immediately** 副 すぐに
- **in** 前 ①《場所・位置・所属》~(の中)に[で・の] ②《時》~(の時)に[の・で], ~後(に), ~の間(に) ③《方法・手段》~で ④~を身につけて, ~を着て ⑤~に関して, ~について ⑥《状態》~の状態で 副 中へ[に], 内へ[に] in fact つまり
- **inside** 名 内部, 内側 副 内部[内側]に 前 ~の内部[内側]に
- **instead** 副 その代わりに instead of ~の代わりに
- **into** 前 ①《動作・運動の方向》~の中へ[に] ②《変化》~に[へ]
- **invisible** 形 目に見えない, 不可視の
- **invite** 動 招待する, 勧める
- **is** 動 be(~である)の3人称単数現在
- **island** 名 島
- **it** 代 ①それは[が], それを[に] ②《天候・日時・距離・寒暖などを示す》
- **its** 代 それの, あれの
- **itself** 代 それ自体, それ自身

J

- **Jack** 名 ジャック《人名》
- **job** 名 仕事, 任務 leave a job 仕事をやめる
- **John** 名 ジョン《人名》
- **join** 動 一緒になる, 参加する
- **joy** 名 喜び
- **jump** 動 跳ぶ jump up and down 飛び跳ねる

English Folk Tales

- **just** 副 ①まさに, ちょうど, (〜した)ばかり ②ほんの, 単に, ただ〜だけ ③ちょっと **just as** 〜と全く同じように, 〜のとおりに

K

- **keep** 動 ①とっておく ②飼う
- **kept** 動 keep (とっておく) の過去, 過去分詞
- **kick** 動 ける, キックする
- **kill** 動 殺す
- **killer** 名 殺し屋, 〜殺し
- **kind** 名 種類 **all kinds of** さまざまな, あらゆる種類の
- **king** 名 王, 国王
- **King Arthur** アーサー王《イギリスの伝説の英雄》
- **kingdom** 名 王国
- **kitchen** 名 台所, 調理場
- **knew** 動 know (知っている) の過去
- **knife** 名 ナイフ, 短剣
- **knight** 名 騎士 **Knight of the Round Table** 円卓の騎士
- **knock** 動 ノックする, たたく 名 戸をたたくこと[音], ノック
- **know** 動 知っている, 知る, (〜が)わかる, 理解している **know better than to** 〜するほどばかではない, 〜しないほうがいいと分かっている
- **known** 形 知られた

L

- **lady** 名 婦人, 淑女
- **laid** 動 lay (卵を産む) の過去, 過去分詞
- **land** 名 陸地, 土地 動 着地する
- **large** 形 ①大きい, 広い ②大勢の, 多量の
- **last** 形 この前の 副 この前 動 続く **at last** ついに, とうとう
- **late** 副 遅く
- **later** 副 後で
- **laugh** 動 笑う
- **laughter** 名 笑い(声)
- **lay** 動 ①卵を産む ②lie (横たわる) の過去
- **learn** 動 知識[経験]を得る **never learn** 懲りない
- **leave** 動 ①〜から離れる, 〜を後にする ②〜をあとに残す, 〜をそのままにしておく **leave a job** 仕事をやめる **left over** 食べ残しの
- **left** 動 leave (去る, 〜をあとに残す) の過去, 過去分詞
- **leg** 名 脚, すね
- **Lent** 名 レント, 四旬節《キリストの受難をしのび断食や修養を行う40日の聖節期間》
- **lesson** 名 教訓, 戒め
- **let** 動 (人に〜)させる, (〜するのを)許す, (〜をある状態に)する **let us** どうか私たちに〜させてください
- **lid** 名 (箱, なべなどの)ふた **put a lid on** 〜にふたをする
- **life** 名 ①生命, 生物 ②一生, 生涯, 人生 ③生活, 暮らし, 世の中 **for the first time in one's life** 生まれて初めて **for the rest of life** この先ずっと
- **lift** 動 持ち上げる
- **light** 名 光, 明かり 動 火をつける
- **like** 動 好む, 好きである 前 〜に似ている, 〜のような 形 似ている, 〜のような 接 あたかも〜のように **feel like** 〜のような感じがする **look like** 〜のように見える **would like to** 〜したいと思う
- **listen** 動 《- to》〜を聞く, 〜に耳を傾ける
- **lit** 動 light (火をつける) の過去, 過

Word List

去分詞

- **little** 形 ①小さい, 幼い ②少しの, 短い **for a little while** しばらくの間
- **live** 動 住む, 暮らす, 生きている **live on one's own** 独り立ちする **not live to see** ~を見ることなく死ぬ
- **lock** 動 錠を下ろす, 閉じ込める **lock someone up** (人を)監禁する
- **London** 名 ロンドン《英国の首都》
- **long** 形 長い, 長期の 副 ずっと **no longer** もはや~でない[~しない] **not~any longer** もはや~でない[~しない]
- **look** 動 ①見る ②(~に)見える, (~の)顔つきをする ③注意する 名 一見, 見ること **get a good look** ~をよく見る **look around** まわりを見回す **look for** ~を探す **look in** 中を見る **look like** ~のように見える **look out** 外を見る **look through** ~をのぞき込む **look up** 見上げる **take a closer look** もう少し近くで見る
- **lose** 動 失う
- **lot** 名《a-of》たくさんの~
- **loud** 形 大声の, 騒がしい 副 大声に[で] **count out loud** 声に出して数える
- **loudly** 副 大声で, 騒がしく
- **lovely** 形 美しい, すばらしい
- **luck** 名 運, 幸運
- **lucky** 形 運のよい
- **lunchtime** 名 お昼時

M

- **made** 動 make (作る)の過去, 過去分詞
- **magic** 形 魔法の, 魔力のある
- **magical** 形 魔法の力による
- **make** 動 ①作る, 得る ②行う, (~に)なる ③(~を…に)する, (~を…)させる **make a climb into** ~に上がっていく **make it** やり遂げる **make noise** 音を立てる **make sure** 確かめる, 確実に~する
- **maker** 名 作り手 **butter maker** バター製造器
- **man** 名 男性, 人
- **many** 形 多数の, たくさんの **so many** 非常に多くの
- **market** 名 市場, マーケット
- **married** 動 marry (結婚する)の過去, 過去分詞
- **marry** 動 結婚する
- **master** 名 主人, 雇い主
- **matter** 名 事件, 問題 **no matter how** どんなに~であろうとも
- **may** 動 ①~かもしれない ②~してもよい, ~できる **May I ~?** ~してもよいですか。
- **maybe** 副 たぶん, おそらく
- **me** 代 私を[に]
- **meal** 名 食事
- **mean** 動 意味する 形 卑怯な, 意地悪な **mean everything to** ~にとって重要な
- **meant** 動 mean (意味する)の過去, 過去分詞
- **meat** 名 肉
- **meet** 動 ①会う, 知り合いになる ②合流する
- **men** 名 man (男性)の複数
- **mention** 動 (~について)述べる, 言及する
- **merry** 形 陽気な, 愉快な
- **Merry Garden** メリーガーデン《地名》
- **message** 名 伝言
- **messenger** 名 使者
- **met** 動 meet (会う)の過去, 過去分詞
- **middle** 名 中間, 最中 **in the**

- middle of ～の真ん中［中ほど］に
- □ **might** 助《mayの過去》①～かもしれない ②～してもよい、～できる
- □ **mile** 名マイル《長さの単位。1,609m》
- □ **mind** 名心、考え
- □ **minute** 名ちょっとの間 at any minute 今にも
- □ **miss** 動（目標を）はずす
- □ **moment** 名瞬間、ちょっとの間 for a moment 少しの間
- □ **money** 名金、通貨
- □ **month** 名月、1ヵ月
- □ **more** 形①もっと多くの ②それ以上の、余分の 副もっと、さらに多く、いっそう more and more ますます no more もう～ない
- □ **morning** 名朝、午前
- □ **most** 副最も
- □ **mother** 名母、母親
- □ **mountain** 名山
- □ **mouth** 名口
- □ **move** 動動く、移動する move on 先に進む
- □ **Mr.** 名《男性に対して》～さん、～氏
- □ **much** 形（量・程度が）多くの、多量の 副とても、たいへん 名多量、たくさん
- □ **music** 名音楽
- □ **must** 助①～しなければならない ②～に違いない
- □ **my** 代私の

N

- □ **name** 名名前
- □ **near** 前～の近くに、～のそばに
- □ **nearby** 形近くの、間近の 副近くで、間近で
- □ **need** 動（～を）必要とする、必要である 助～する必要がある 名必要（性） in need 困窮している need to do ～する必要がある
- □ **neighbor** 名隣人
- □ **nervous** 形神経が高ぶった、緊張した
- □ **never** 副決して［少しも］～ない、一度も［二度と］～ない never learn 懲りない
- □ **new** 形新しい、新鮮な
- □ **news** 名知らせ、ニュース
- □ **next** 形①次の、翌～ ②隣の 副①次に ②隣に next to ～の隣に
- □ **nice** 形すてきな、よい、親切な
- □ **nicely** 副親切に
- □ **night** 名夜、晩
- □ **no** 副①いいえ、いや ②少しも～ない 形～がない、少しも～ない、～どころでない、～禁止 no longer もはや～でない［～しない］ no matter how どんなに～であろうとも no more もう～ない no one 誰もseed[一人も］～ない no one else 他の誰一人として～しない
- □ **noise** 名騒音、物音 make noise 音を立てる
- □ **none** 代（～の）何も［誰も・少しも］…ない
- □ **nose** 名鼻
- □ **not** 副～でない、～しない not～ any longer もはや～でない［～しない］ not～but… ～ではなくて… Not by the hair of my chinny-chin-chin あごひげにかけて絶対やだね《言葉遊び的表現》
- □ **nothing** 代何も～ない
- □ **Nottingham** 名ノッティンガム《地名》
- □ **now** 副①今（では）、現在 ②今すぐに 名今、現在 from now on 今後
- □ **number** 名数 a number of 多くの～

WORD LIST

O

- **object** 名物体
- **o'clock** 副〜時
- **of** 前①《所有・所属・部分》〜の,〜に属する ②《性質・特徴・材料》〜の,〜製の ③《部分》〜のうち ④《分離・除去》〜から **of course** もちろん,当然
- **off** 副①離れて ②はずれて 前〜を離れて,〜をはずれて **off to**（今いる場所を離れて）〜に向かう
- **office** 名執務室,事務所
- **oh** 間ああ,おや,まあ
- **OK** 形《許可・同意・満足などを表して》よろしい,いいよ
- **old** 形①年取った,老いた ②〜歳の ③古い,昔の
- **on** 前①《場所・接触》〜（の上）に ②《日・時》〜に,〜と同時に,〜のすぐ後で ③《関係・従事》〜に関して,〜について,〜して 副①身につけて,上に ②前へ,続けて
- **once** 副①一度,1回 ②かつて 名一度,1回 接いったん〜すると **once and for all** きっぱりと **once upon a time** むかしむかし
- **one** 名1（の数字）,1人［個］ 形①1の,1人［個］の ②ある〜 ③《the 〜》唯一の 代①（一般の）人,ある物 ②一方,片方 ③〜なもの **no one** 誰も［一人も］〜ない **no one else** 他の誰一人として〜しない **one after another** 次々に,1つ［人］ずつ **one day** ある日 **one of** 〜の1つ［人］
- **only** 形唯一の 副①〜にすぎない,ただ〜だけ ②やっと
- **onto** 前〜の上へ［に］
- **open** 動開く,開ける
- **or** 接①〜か…,または ②さもないと ③すなわち,言い換えると **or else** さもないと
- **order** 動（〜するよう）命じる
- **other** 形①ほかの,異なった ②（2つのうち）もう一方の,（3つ以上のうち）残りの **each other** お互いに
- **our** 代私たちの
- **out** 副①外へ［に］,不在で,離れて ②世に出て ③消えて ④すっかり 形①外の,公表された ②公表された 前〜から外へ［に］,〜から抜け出して,〜の範囲外に **way out** 脱出方法,解決法
- **outside** 名外部,外側 副外へ,外側に
- **oven** 名かまど,オーブン
- **over** 前①〜の上の［に］,〜を一面に覆って ②〜を越えて,〜以上に,〜よりまさって ③〜の向こう側の［に］ ④〜の間 副上に,一面に,ずっと 形①上部の,上位の,過多の ②終わって,すんで **all over** 〜中で,全体にわたって,〜の至る所で **over and over again** 何度も繰り返して
- **ow** 間痛い,あいたっ
- **own** 形自身の **live on one's own** 独り立ちする

P

- **pain** 名痛み
- **part** 名部分
- **pass** 動（年月が）たつ
- **past** 前《場所》〜を過ぎて,〜を越して
- **pay** 動①支払う,払う ②償う
- **people** 名人々,民衆
- **perhaps** 副たぶん,ことによると
- **person** 名①人 ②人格,人柄
- **Peter** 名ピーター《人名》
- **pick** 動（〜を）摘み取る **pick up** 拾い上げる
- **pie** 名パイ
- **piece** 名一片
- **pig** 名ブタ（豚）

- □ **pile** 名積み重ね, (〜の)山
- □ **place** 名①場所, 建物 ②空間 動置く, 収納する
- □ **plan** 名計画, 案 動計画する **plan to do** 〜するつもりである
- □ **plant** 名植物, 草木 動植えつける
- □ **play** 動(楽器を)演奏する
- □ **please** 副どうか, お願いだから 間①どうぞ ②お願いします
- □ **pocket** 名ポケット
- □ **pond** 名池
- □ **poor** 形①貧しい, 粗末な ②不幸な, 気の毒な 名《the –》貧民
- □ **pot** 名壺, (深い)なべ
- □ **potato** 名ジャガイモ
- □ **power** 名力, 能力
- □ **prepare** 動準備[用意]をする
- □ **presence** 名存在すること
- □ **pretty** 形かわいい, きれいな
- □ **priest** 名聖職者, 牧師
- □ **prisoner** 名捕虜, 拘束された人
- □ **probably** 副たぶん
- □ **promise** 名約束 動約束する
- □ **protect** 動守る, 保護する
- □ **punish** 動罰する, ひどい目にあわせる
- □ **put** 動①置く, のせる ②入れる, つける ③(ある状態に)する ④putの過去, 過去分詞 **put a lid on** 〜にふたをする **put back** (もとの場所に)戻す, 返す **put on** ①〜を身につける, 着る ②〜を…の上に置く **put 〜 in 〜** を…の中に入れる **put 〜 into 〜** を…に突っ込む

Q

- □ **question** 名質問, 疑問
- □ **quickly** 副敏速に, 急いで
- □ **quiet** 形静かな, じっとした
- □ **quietly** 副静かに

R

- □ **rain** 名雨
- □ **raise** 動(高く)持ち上げる
- □ **ran** 動run (走る)の過去
- □ **reach** 動着く, 到着する
- □ **read** 動読む, 〜と書いてある
- □ **ready** 形用意[準備]ができた, まさに〜しようとする, 今にも〜せんばかりの **be ready to** すぐに[いつでも]〜できる, 〜する構えで
- □ **realize** 動〜に気づく
- □ **really** 副本当に, 確かに
- □ **recently** 副近ごろ, 最近
- □ **recognize** 動識別する, (人を)覚えている
- □ **red** 形赤い
- □ **rejoice** 動喜ぶ
- □ **relax** 動くつろぐ
- □ **release** 動解放する
- □ **remain** 動(〜の)ままである[いる]
- □ **remember** 動思い出す, 覚えている
- □ **rest** 名《the 〜》残り 動休む, 眠る **for the rest of life** この先ずっと
- □ **result** 名結果 **as a result** その結果(として)
- □ **return** 動帰る, 戻る 名帰還 **return to** 〜に戻る, 〜に帰る
- □ **rich** 形金持ちの 名《-es》財産, 富
- □ **ridden** 動ride (乗る)の過去分詞
- □ **ride** 動馬に乗る **ride away** 馬に乗って去る
- □ **right** 形正しい, 適切な 副①まっすぐに, すぐに ②ちょうど, 正確に **right away** すぐに **right down to** 〜まで徹底的に **walk right up behind**

Word List

〜のすぐ後ろに歩み寄る
- **ring** 名 指輪
- **river** 名 川
- **roar** 動 ①ほえる ②（人が）わめく 名 ほえ声, 怒号
- **rock** 名 岩, 岩石
- **rode** 動 ride（乗る）の過去
- **roll** 動 転がる　roll down 転がり落ちる
- **room** 名 部屋
- **rope** 名 なわ, ロープ
- **round** 形 丸い, 円形の　Knight of the Round Table 円卓の騎士
- **run** 動 走る　run after 〜を追いかける　run around 走り回る　run away 走り去る, 逃げ出す　run away from 〜から逃れる　run out of 〜を使い果たす　run over 〜の上を走る　run up 〜に走り寄る

S

- **sad** 形 悲しい, 悲しげな
- **safe** 形 安全な, 危険のない
- **safely** 副 安全に
- **said** 動 say（言う）の過去, 過去分詞
- **same** 形 同じ, 同様の
- **sat** 動 sit（座る）の過去, 過去分詞
- **save** 動 救う, 守る
- **saw** 動 see（見る）の過去
- **say** 動 言う, 口に出す　名 言うこと　say to oneself ひとり言を言う, 心に思う
- **scare** 動 ①（人を）怖がらせる ②怖がる
- **scared** 形 おびえた, びっくりした　be scared of 〜を恐れる
- **scary** 形 恐ろしい
- **scream** 動 叫ぶ, 金切り声を出す
- **search** 動 捜し求める, 調べる 名 探索　in search of 〜を探し求めて
- **seat** 動 着席させる　seat oneself 席に着く
- **second** 名 （時間の）秒, 瞬時 形 第2の, 2番の
- **secret** 形 秘密の
- **see** 動 ①見る, 見える, 見物する ②（〜と）わかる, 認識する, 経験する ③会う ④考える, 確かめる, 調べる ⑤気をつける　not live to see 〜を見ることなく死ぬ　see if 〜かどうかを確かめる
- **seem** 動 （〜に）見える, （〜のように）思われる
- **seen** 動 see（見る）の過去分詞
- **sell** 動 売る
- **send** 動 ①送る, 届ける ②手紙を出す ③（人を〜に）行かせる ④《−＋人［物など］＋-ing》〜を（ある状態に）する　send〜along 〜を送り届ける　send out 送り出す
- **sense** 名 分別, 判断能力
- **sent** 動 send（送る）の過去, 過去分詞
- **servant** 名 召使, 使用人
- **set** 動 ①（〜を…の状態に）する, させる ②setの過去, 過去分詞　set off 出発する　set out 出発する
- **several** 形 それぞれの
- **shake** 動 揺れる, 震える
- **shall** 助 ①《Iが主語で》〜するだろう, 〜だろう ②《I以外が主語で》（…に）〜させよう, （…は）〜することになるだろう
- **shape** 名 形, 姿
- **share** 動 分配する, 共有する
- **she** 代 彼女は［が］
- **sheep** 名 羊
- **ship** 名 船
- **shoe** 名 《-s》靴
- **shook** 動 shake（震える）の過去
- **short** 形 短い

- □ **should** 助 ～すべきである，～したほうがよい
- □ **shoulder** 名 肩
- □ **shout** 動 叫ぶ，どなりつける
- □ **shovel** 名 シャベル
- □ **show** 動 ①見せる，示す ②案内する
- □ **sick** 形 病気の
- □ **side** 名 側面，横 turn ～ on its side ～を横向きにする
- □ **silver** 名 銀，銀貨
- □ **since** 接 ～だから
- □ **sing** 動 歌う，さえずる
- □ **single** 形 それぞれの every single day 一日も欠かさずに
- □ **sir** 名 あなた，だんなさま《目上の男性，客などに対する呼びかけ》
- □ **sit** 動 座る sit on ～に腰をかける
- □ **six** 名 6(の数字)
- □ **sixth** 形 第6番目の
- □ **sky** 名 空，天空
- □ **sleep** 動 眠る，寝る sleep in ～で寝る
- □ **slept** 動 sleep(眠る)の過去，過去分詞
- □ **slowly** 副 ゆっくりと
- □ **small** 形 小さい
- □ **smart** 形 利口な，抜け目のない
- □ **smell** 動 (～の)においを感じる
- □ **smile** 動 微笑する，にっこり笑う 名 微笑，ほほえみ
- □ **Smith** 名 スミス《人名》
- □ **sneak** 動 こそこそする sneak out of ～から抜け出す
- □ **so** 副 ①とても ②同様に，～もまた ③《先行する句・節の代用》そのように，そう 接 ①だから，それで ②では，さて and so そこで，それだから so many 非常に多くの so that ～するために，それで，～できるように so ～that 非常に～なので…

- □ **soft** 形 温和な，落ち着いた
- □ **sold** 動 sell(売る)の過去，過去分詞
- □ **solid** 形 (金などが)中まで同じ材質の，純粋の
- □ **some** 形 ①いくつかの，多少の ②ある，誰か，何か 代 ①いくつか ②ある人[物]たち
- □ **someone** 代 ある人，誰か
- □ **something** 代 ある物，何か something to do 何か～すべきこと
- □ **son** 名 息子
- □ **song** 名 歌
- □ **soon** 副 まもなく，すぐに
- □ **sorry** 形 気の毒に[申し訳なく]思う
- □ **sound** 動 (～のように)思われる，(～と)聞こえる
- □ **soundly** 副 ぐっすりと，完全に
- □ **special** 形 特別の，特殊な
- □ **spell** 名 呪文，(呪文の)魔力
- □ **spend** 動 (時を)過ごす
- □ **spent** 動 spend(時を過ごす)の過去，過去分詞
- □ **spot** 名 地点，場所 動 ～を見つける
- □ **stab** 動 (突き)刺す
- □ **stalk** 名 (植物の)茎
- □ **stand** 動 立つ stand by そばに立つ
- □ **start** 動 ①始まる，始める ②生じる，生じさせる start a fire 火をつける start to do ～し始める
- □ **stay** 動 ①とどまる，泊まる，滞在する ②持続する，(～の)ままでいる stay in (場所)に泊まる，滞在する stay on 居残る，とどまる stay with ～の所に泊まる
- □ **steal** 動 盗む
- □ **step** 名 歩み，1歩
- □ **stick** 名 棒，枝木 動 (止まったまま)

Word List

動かない, 立ち往生する
- □ **still** 副 ①まだ, 今でも ②それでも (なお)
- □ **stole** 動 steal (盗む) の過去
- □ **stolen** 動 steal (盗む) の過去分詞
- □ **stood** 動 stand (立つ) の過去, 過去分詞
- □ **stop** 動 やめる **stop doing** 〜するのをやめる
- □ **story** 名 物語, 話
- □ **strange** 形 奇妙な, 変わった
- □ **straw** 名 麦わら
- □ **strength** 名 力 **with all the strength** ありったけの力で
- □ **strong** 形 強い, 堅固な
- □ **stuck** 動 stick (刺さる) の過去, 過去分詞 形 立ち往生した, 行きづまった **be stuck** 身動きが取れない
- □ **such** 形 そんなに, とても **such 〜 that** 非常に〜なので…
- □ **sudden** 形 突然の, 急な **all of a sudden** 突然, 前触れもなしに
- □ **suddenly** 副 突然, 急に
- □ **sun** 名 《the –》太陽, 日
- □ **sure** 形 確かな, 確実な, 《be – to》必ず [きっと] 〜する, 確信して 副 確かに, まったく, 本当に **for sure** 確かに, 確実に **make sure** 確かめる, 確実に〜する **not sure if** 〜かどうかわからない **sure enough** 確かに
- □ **surely** 副 間違いなく
- □ **surprise** 動 驚かす, 不意に襲う
- □ **surprised** 動 surprise (驚かす) の過去, 過去分詞 形 驚いた **be surprised to do** 〜して驚く
- □ **swim** 動 泳ぐ
- □ **swing** 動 〜を振る 名 打つこと **take a swing** 一撃を加える
- □ **sword** 名 剣, 刀
- □ **swung** 動 swing (振る) の過去, 過去分詞

T

- □ **table** 名 テーブル, 食卓 **Knight of the Round Table** 円卓の騎士
- □ **take** 動 ①取る, 持つ ②持って [連れて] いく, 捕らえる ③乗る ④(時間・労力を) 費やす, 必要とする ⑤(ある動作を) する ⑥飲む ⑦耐える, 受け入れる **take a closer look** もう少し近くで見る **take a swing** 一撃を加える **take away** 取り除く **take care of** 〜の世話をする, 〜の面倒を見る **take out** 取り出す **take someone in** 〜を家に泊めてやる **take 〜 off** 〜を取り去る **take 〜 out of** 〜を…から出す **take 〜 to** 〜を…に連れて [持って] 行く
- □ **taken** 動 take (取る) の過去分詞
- □ **tale** 名 話, 物語
- □ **talk** 動 話す, 相談する **talk of** 〜のことを話す
- □ **tall** 形 高い, 背の高い
- □ **teach** 動 教える
- □ **tell** 動 話す, 言う, 教える
- □ **terrible** 形 恐ろしい, ひどい, ものすごい
- □ **terribly** 副 ひどく
- □ **than** 接 〜よりも, 〜以上に
- □ **thank** 動 感謝する, 礼を言う **thank god** ありがたい **thank 〜 for** 〜に対して…の礼を言う **thank goodness** ありがたい, よかった
- □ **that** 形 その, あの 代 ①それ, あれ, その [あの] 人 [物] ②《関係代名詞》〜である… 接 〜ということ, 〜なので, 〜だから 副 そんなに, それほど **so that** 〜するために, それで, 〜できるように
- □ **the** 冠 ①その, あの ②《形容詞の前で》〜な人々 副 《– +比較級, – +比較級》〜すればするほど…
- □ **their** 代 彼 (女) らの, それらの
- □ **them** 代 彼 (女) らを [に], それらを [に]

117

- **themselves** 代 彼(女)ら自身, それら自身
- **then** 副 その時(に・は), それから, 次に 名 その時 形 その当時の
- **there** ①そこに[で・の], そこへ, あそこへ ②《~ is [are]》~がある[いる] 名 そこ **there is no way ~** する見込みはない
- **these** 代 これら, これ 形 これらの, この
- **they** 代 ①彼(女)らは[が], それらは[が] ②(一般の)人々は[が]
- **thick** 形 分厚い, がっしりした
- **thing** 名 ①物, 事 ②《-s》事情, 事柄
- **think** 動 思う, 考える **think of ~** のことを考える, ~を思いつく
- **third** 形 第3の, 3番の
- **this** 形 ①この, こちらの, これを ②今の, 現在の 代 ①これ, この人[物] ②今, ここ **this way** このように **to this day** 今日に至るまで
- **those** 形 それらの, あれらの 代 それらの人[物]
- **though** 接 ①~にもかかわらず, ~だが ②たとえ~でも 副 しかし **even though** ~にもかかわらず
- **thought** 動 think (思う)の過去, 過去分詞
- **three** 名 3(の数字) 形 3の
- **threw** 動 throw (投げる)の過去
- **through** 前 ~を通り抜けて, ~を通って
- **throw** 動 投げる **throw off** 脱ぎ捨てる **throw ~ down** ~を投げ下ろす
- **Thunderdel** 名 サンダーデル《人名》
- **tie** 動 結ぶ, 束縛する **tie up** ひもで縛る, 縛り上げる
- **time** 名 ①時, 時間, 歳月 ②時期, 時代 ③期間 ④回, 倍 **every time** ~するときはいつも, ~のたびに **for the first time in one's life** 生まれて初めて **have no time to do** ~する時間がない **once upon a time** むかしむかし
- **tired** 形 ①疲れた ②あきた
- **to** 前 ①《方向・変化》~へ, ~に, ~の方へ ②《程度・時間》~まで ③《適合・付加・所属》~に ④《-+動詞の原形》~するために[の], ~する, ~すること **to this day** 今日に至るまで
- **today** 副 今日(では)
- **together** 副 ①一緒に ②同時に
- **told** 動 tell (話す)の過去, 過去分詞
- **tomorrow** 名 明日 副 明日は
- **tonight** 名 今夜, 今晩 副 今夜は
- **too** 副 ①~も(また) ②あまりに~すぎる, とても~
- **took** 動 take (取る)の過去
- **tool** 名 道具, 工具
- **top** 名 頂上 副 **on top of ~** ~の上(部)に
- **toward** 前 《運動の方向・位置》~の方へ, ~に向かって
- **town** 名 町, 都市
- **townspeople** 名 市民, 町民
- **travel** 動 ①旅行する, 移動する ②伝わる
- **treasure** 名 財宝, 宝物
- **tree** 名 樹木
- **trick** 動 だます
- **tried** 動 try (試みる)の過去, 過去分詞
- **trip** 名 (短い)旅行, 遠征
- **trouble** 名 ①もめごと ②苦労 **get in trouble** 厄介ごとに巻き込まれる, 災難に見舞われる **have trouble ~** するのに苦労する
- **trumpet** 名 ラッパ, トランペット
- **try** 動 ①やってみる, 試みる ②努力する
- **tumble** 動 倒れる, 転ぶ

Word List

- **turn** 動 ①ひっくり返す, 回転する[させる], 曲がる, 曲げる, 向かう, 向ける ②(～に)なる, (～に)変える **turn back** 元に戻る[戻す] **turn into** ～に変わる[変える] **turn to** ～の方を向く **turn ～ on its side** ～を横向きにする
- **twelve** 名 12 (の数字)
- **two** 名 2 (の数字) 形 2の **break in two** 二つに折れる

U

- **uncle** 名 おじ
- **under** 前 ①《位置》～の下[に] ②《状態》～で, ～を受けて, ～のもと
- **unlock** 動 かぎを開ける
- **until** 前 ～まで(ずっと) 接 ～の時まで, ～するまで
- **unusual** 形 普通でない
- **up** 副 ①上へ, 上がって, 北へ ②立って, 近づいて ③向上して, 増して 前 ①～の上(の方)へ, 高い方へ ②(道)に沿って 形 上向きの, 上りの **up to** ～まで, ～に至るまで
- **upon** 前 ①《場所・接触》～(の上)に ②《日・時》～に ③《関係・従事》～に関して, ～について, ～して 副 前へ, 続けて **once upon a time** むかしむかし
- **upset** 形 憤慨して, 動揺して 動 気を悪くさせる, (心・神経など)をかき乱す
- **urge** 動 《– someone to》(人に)～するよう熱心に勧める
- **us** 代 私たちを[に]
- **use** 動 使う, 用いる
- **used** 動 use (使う) の過去, 過去分詞

V

- **very** 副 とても, 非常に 形 本当の, まさしくその
- **village** 名 村, 村落
- **visit** 動 訪問する
- **voice** 名 声

W

- **wait** 動 待つ, 《– for》～を待つ
- **wake** 動 起きる, 起こす **wake up** 起きる, 目を覚ます
- **Wales** 名 ウェールズ《英国南西部の地方》
- **walk** 動 歩く, 歩かせる, 散歩する **walk around** 歩き回る **walk away** 立ち去る **walk on** 歩き続ける **walk over to** ～まで歩いていく **walk right up behind** ～のすぐ後ろに歩み寄る **walk to** ～まで歩いて行く **walk up to** ～に歩み寄る
- **wall** 名 壁
- **wand** 名 杖
- **want** 動 ほしい, ～したい, ～してほしい
- **warm** 形 暖かい
- **was** 動 《be の第1・第3人称単数現在 am, is の過去》～であった, (～に)いた[あった]
- **waste** 動 浪費する
- **watch** 動 ①じっと見る, 見物する ②注意[用心]する, 監視する **watch over** 見守る
- **water** 名 ①水 ②(川・湖・海などの)多量の水
- **way** 名 ①道, 通り道 ②方向, 距離 ③方法, 手段 ④習慣 **continue on one's way** 歩き続ける **find one's way out** 解決策を見いだす **go on one's way** 道を進む **in this way** このようにして **on one's way** (目的地への) 途中で **on one's way to** ～に

行く途中で **there is no way** 〜する見込みはない **this way** このように **way out** 脱出方法, 解決法 **way to 〜** する方法

- **we** 代 私たちは[が]
- **weaken** 動 弱める
- **wear** 動 着る, 身につける
- **weather** 名 天気, 天候
- **wedding** 名 結婚式, 婚礼
- **welcome** 形 歓迎の, 遠慮不要の **you are welcome** どういたしまして
- **well** 副 ①うまく, 上手に ②しっかりと 間 へえ, おや
- **went** 動 go（行く）の過去
- **were** 動 《be の 2 人称単数・複数の過去》〜であった, (〜に)いた[あった]
- **what** 代 ①何が [を・に] ②《関係代名詞》〜するところのもの[こと] 形 ①何の, どんな ②なんと ③〜するだけの 副 いかに, どれほど **guess what** 一体何なのか当ててみる
- **when** 副 ①いつ ②《関係副詞》〜するところの, 〜するとその時, 〜するとき 接 〜の時, 〜するとき 代 いつ
- **whenever** 接 〜するたびに, いつ〜しても
- **where** 副 ①どこに[で] ②《関係副詞》〜するところの, そしてそこで, 〜するところ 接 〜なところに[へ], 〜するところに[へ] 代 ①どこ, どの点 ②〜するところの
- **wherever** 接 どこでも, どこへ[で]〜するとも
- **whether** 接 〜であろうとなかろうと
- **whew** 間 ヒャー！, ひゅー, やれやれ
- **which** 形 どちらの, どの 代 《関係代名詞》〜するところの
- **while** 接 少しの時間 **for a little while** しばらくの間
- **whistle** 動 (口) 笛を吹く
- **white** 形 白い
- **who** 代 ①誰が[は], どの人 ②《関係代名詞》〜するところの(人)
- **whole** 形 全体の, すべての
- **whose** 代 《関係代名詞》(〜の)…するところの
- **why** 副 なぜ, どうして 間 おや, まあ
- **wide** 形 幅が〜ある 副 すっかり
- **wife** 名 妻, 夫人
- **will** 助 〜だろう, 〜しよう, する(つもりだ)
- **wind** 名 風
- **window** 名 窓
- **wine** 名 ワイン, ぶどう酒
- **wise** 形 賢い
- **wish** 動 望む, 願う 名 (心からの)願い
- **with** 前 ①《同伴・付随・所属》〜と一緒に, 〜を身につけて, 〜とともに ②《様態》〜(の状態)で, 〜して ③《手段・道具》〜で, 〜を使って
- **without** 前 〜しないで
- **woke** 動 wake（目が覚める）の過去
- **wolf** 名 オオカミ（狼）
- **woman** 名 (成人した) 女性, 婦人
- **women** 名 woman（女性）の複数
- **wonder** 動 不思議に思う, (〜に)驚く **wonder if** 〜ではないかと思う
- **wonderful** 形 驚くべき, すばらしい, すてきな
- **won't** will not の短縮形
- **wood** 名 ①《しばしば -s》森, 林 ②木材
- **wooden** 形 木製の
- **wore** 動 wear（着ている）の過去
- **work** 動 働く 名 仕事
- **world** 名 《the 〜》世界
- **worried** 動 worry（悩む）の過去,

Word List

過去分詞
- **worry** 動 心配する[させる] worry about ~のことを心配する
- **would** 助《willの過去》①~するだろう、~するつもりだ ②~したものだ would like to ~したいと思う
- **wrong** 副 間違って

Y

- **year** 名 ①年、1年 ②~歳 all year 一年中、一年を通して for years and years 何年もの間 for ~ years ~年間、~年にわたって
- **yell** 動 大声をあげる、わめく
- **yes** 副 はい、そうです
- **York** 名 ヨーク《地名》
- **you** 代 ①あなた(方)は[が]、あなた(方)を[に] ②(一般に)人は
- **young** 形 若い
- **your** 代 あなた(方)の
- **yours** 代 あなた(方)のもの

English Conversational Ability Test
国際英語会話能力検定

● E-CATとは…
英語が話せるようになるためのテストです。インターネットベースで、30分であなたの発話力をチェックします。

www.ecatexam.com

● iTEP®とは…
世界各国の企業、政府機関、アメリカの大学300校以上が、英語能力判定テストとして採用。オンラインによる90分のテストで文法、リーディング、リスニング、ライティング、スピーキングの5技能をスコア化。iTEP®は、留学、就職、海外赴任などに必要な、世界に通用する英語力を総合的に評価する画期的なテストです。

www.itepexamjapan.com

ラダーシリーズ
English Folk Tales イギリス民話

2018年11月 4日　第1刷発行
2025年 6月20日　第2刷発行

リライト　　エマ・サリー

発行者　　賀川　　洋

発行所　　IBCパブリッシング株式会社
　　　　　〒162-0804 東京都新宿区中里町29番3号
　　　　　菱秀神楽坂ビル
　　　　　Tel. 03-3513-4511　Fax. 03-3513-4512
　　　　　www.ibcpub.co.jp

© IBC Publishing, Inc. 2018

印刷　株式会社シナノパブリッシングプレス
装丁　伊藤 理恵　　カバーイラスト　Mildred Lyon
組版データ　Sabon Roman + Gotham Bold

落丁本・乱丁本は、小社宛にお送りください。送料小社負担にてお取り替えいたします。本書の無断複写（コピー）は著作権法上での例外を除き禁じられています。

Printed in Japan
ISBN978-4-7946-0563-4